Hollywood and Intimacy

Hollywood and Intimacy

Style, Moments, Magnificence

Steven Peacock

First published 2012 by
PALGRAVE MACMILLAN

Palgrave Macmillan in the UK is an imprint of Macmillan Publishers Limited, registered in England, company number 785998, of Houndmills, Basingstoke, Hampshire RG21 6XS.

Palgrave Macmillan in the US is a division of St Martin's Press LLC, 175 Fifth Avenue, New York, NY 10010.

Palgrave Macmillan is the global academic imprint of the above companies and has companies and representatives throughout the world.

Palgrave® and Macmillan® are registered trademarks in the United States, the United Kingdom, Europe and other countries.

ISBN 978–0–230–35450–0

This book is printed on paper suitable for recycling and made from fully managed and sustained forest sources. Logging, pulping and manufacturing processes are expected to conform to the environmental regulations of the country of origin.

A catalogue record for this book is available from the British Library.

A catalog record for this book is available from the Library of Congress.

10   9   8   7   6   5   4   3   2   1
21   20   19   18   17   16   15   14   13   12

Printed and bound in Great Britain by
CPI Antony Rowe, Chippenham and Eastbourne

For Leigh, and my parents.

Contents

List of Figures

Acknowledgements

Thank you first and foremost to Andrew Klevan for his support, guidance, and friendship. From the very beginnings of this book's development, his encouragement has been instrumental in helping me think through ideas. To all at Palgrave Macmillan, and especially Felicity Plester: thank you. Your enthusiasm for the project proved invaluable to its realisation. Thank you too to Edward Gallafent, John Gibbs, and Douglas Pye, for detailed and insightful comments across the drafts. I would also like to thank fellow scholars previously gathered in olden golden times at the University of Kent: Sarah Cardwell, Alex Clayton, Rob Greens, Gary Bettinson, David Turner, Gina Marden, Nigel Mather, B. F. Taylor, and Thalia Baldwin. The Greengrass family's friendship is a gift to treasure. Thank you too to David Scorey and Matthew Roach for the generosity of their time and many conversations. I thank my colleagues at the University of Hertfordshire for their enthusiastic backing, and the AHRC for its source of financial support.

Introduction

Matters of scale

There is a tendency in Film Studies to bemoan the output of contemporary Hollywood in terms of scale. Problems are seen to stem from both the vastness of the current day Hollywood system (the industry), and the shaping of contemporary American film as spectacle (the image). In terms of its industrial sway, concern is raised over Hollywood's global domination, with emphasis on its control of the overseas market. In *Global Hollywood*, Toby Miller considers how 'Hollywood owns between 40 per cent and 90 per cent of the movies shown in the world' and how 'Los Angeles-New York culture and commerce dominate screen entertainment around the globe' (2001: 3–4). Equally, importance is placed on Hollywood's current involvement and position in 'vertically-integrated media conglomerates', in which the major studios 'serve as the base to dominate a plethora of media industries – from television to film, from home video to cable TV, from publishing to theme parks' (Gomery 2000: 52–3).

Hollywood's control of the marketplace is reinforced by the phenomenal success and domineering presence of its big-budget productions. Geoff King describes the predominant visual form of contemporary Hollywood as comprising the 'epic landscape to sumptuous interior ... [of] expansive vistas spread out across the width of the big screen, their presence magnified by the aural impact of multi-channel sound' (2000: 1). Moreover, Hollywood's weighty corporate interests are seen to inform the shape and content of its films. King notes that, 'in an age in which the big Hollywood studios have become absorbed into giant conglomerates, the prevalence of spectacle and spatial effects has been boosted by a growing demand for products that can be further exploited in multimedia forms such as computer games and theme-park rides – secondary outlets that sometimes generate more profits than the films on which they are based' (1–2). Corporate investment, considerations of secondary outlets and the 'prevalence of spectacle' lead to a pervasiveness of large-scale blockbuster movies. As Sheldon Hall comments, 'While at one time blockbusters were distinguished partly by their exceptionalism, their status as an economic category different from and "above" from the normal run of releases, it now seems possible to believe that Hollywood makes nothing *but* blockbusters' (2002: 11). Again, it is not only the dominance but also the scale of the films that causes concern. Critics lament the 'Age of the blockbuster' as bringing a glut of 'large-scale, impersonal Hollywood productions' (Honeycutt 2005) and 'disappointing exercise[s] in overindulgence' (Kay 2006).

Problems of size and scale are not only restricted to the contemporary blockbuster. So-called 'prestige films' such as *Heat* (Michael Mann, 1995) are seen to exhibit forms of 'widescreen largesse', symptomatic of the 'highly polished New Hollywood cinema multiplex audiences flocked to in the 1980s and 1990s' (James 2002: 29). Even Hollywood features that appear to carry 'independent' credentials come under similar criticism. For example, Kent Jones describes *Magnolia* (Paul Thomas Anderson, 2000) as 'sprawling' and as a 'big, self-important, overreaching, but fundamentally sweet picture that fancies itself a major achievement' (2000: 33). This is a rather different kind of largesse to that displayed in either the blockbuster or the prestige picture, suggesting heavy measures of pretentiousness and portentousness; all connect, however, in terms of *indulgence*. Industrially and aesthetically, contemporary Hollywood is seen to carry too much weight. The vocabulary of the academics and critics quoted here evokes a Hollywood at once powerful yet boorish in its inflated state. Gavin Smith encapsulates the mood when he speaks of the 'nineties cul-de-sac of bloated, corrupt mediocrity' (1999: 58). While acknowledging the presence of much 'mediocrity' in terms of recent American cinematic output, this book negotiates a route around the 'cul-de-sac'. It sees the inflated or 'bloated' state of contemporary Hollywood as constituting a *possibility* for the period.

It brings to light a particular stylistic relationship that exists precisely because of the grand scale of contemporary American cinema.

The little within the big

This book shows how a certain group of films uses the grandeur and sweep of contemporary Hollywood cinema to create expressions of intimacy. The films are seen to exhibit a particular rhetoric of expression, drawing on the relationship between 'the big' and 'the little'. In terms of style and structure, an observation by Raymond Durgnat acts as catalyst to the following considerations, what he alludes to as the 'big architecture' of a film. Durgnat sees the arrangements of human motion in the 'wide vistas' and 'panorama shots' of narrative cinema as comprising 'kinetic architecture' (2002: 72–3). He uses the example of the 'acute geometry' of moving cars and people in *Psycho* (Alfred Hitchcock, 1960), as Marion Crane (Janet Leigh) hurriedly buys a replacement vehicle from the car salesman and the curious cop observes from across the street: 'The human figures, their movements, their turning looks, are very precisely "sited", like moving architectural units. It's a tensely organised space-and-motion nexus. Long sight-lines stretch across this wide vista (which contrasts between the messy little spaces through which Marion has been moving)' (73). Panoramic landscapes; wide and long shots; long sight-lines; movements across wide vistas; moments when a film broadens its horizon from 'messy little spaces': these are the components, for Durgnat, of a film's 'big architecture'.

For the purposes of this book, the key claim comes in Durgnat's thoughts on the predominant effects of 'big architecture' in narrative film: 'All too often "big architecture" *dwarfs* a film's characters; makes them small, remote and cold' (73). In contrast, *Psycho*'s 'big outward scene conveys the enormity of Marion's distraction, about her mental lapse' (73). Durgnat continues by alluding briefly to Michelangelo Antonioni's interest in similar stylistic strategies, of 'finding new ways to relate "architectural" long shots, mental states, micro-events and uncertainties' (73–4). Characteristically broad yet penetrating, these observations allude to atypical achievements in cinema, of a filmmaker arranging elements of 'big architecture' in close relationship with a work's characters.

These claims encourage a closer look at film's 'big architecture' and at other, more recent cases, lying outside the 'all too often'. They promote a test of an alternative possibility, that rather than creating 'remote and cold' characterisation, the constituents of a contemporary film's 'big architecture' might also be capable of rendering expressions of human closeness. This book extends beyond the structural supports of 'big architecture' to explore other grades of intimacy afforded by seemingly more diminutive elements of film style (such as details of gesture, sound, and décor). Crucially, though, such elements are taken as a part of the films' larger designs, bound into the bigger picture, often responsible for the dramatic weight of an intimate moment. So, the following readings respond to two overarching notions. First, that the grand gestures of modern American cinema can be seen to facilitate expressions of intimacy. Second, that a sensitive handling of large-scale concerns allows little details to be brought out in a certain way. All of the films considered in the following chapters are exemplary of the way modern American cinema can use its own expansiveness, to shape and exhibit delicate points of entry into the subtleties and complexities of human negotiations.

Four films

In order to get into the details and intricacies of 'intimate Hollywood' – how the modern American movie can use its 'big architecture' to express aspects of closeness – I limit the analysis to four exemplary films. The films are *The Age of Innocence* (Martin Scorsese, 1993), *The Bridges of Madison County* (Clint Eastwood, 1995), *The Insider* (Michael Mann, 1999), and *The Straight Story* (David Lynch, 1999). In different ways, each of these films creates a complex and sophisticated study of human relationships. They explore the intimacy developing between characters, between characters and their environments, and within enclosed communities. Through close analysis, this book unlocks these intimate associations. While the four films under scrutiny are not blockbusters, they can all be sensibly described as 'big' movies. They are crafted with the aid of sizeable budgets; all four are heralded as prestige pictures for major studios; all function with the involvement of 'big name' directors and actors.[1] Moreover, and as key to this study, in temporal and spatial measures, all four films present stories that are at once intimate and extensive.

The Age of Innocence charts a clandestine relationship over decades and in many different grand settings of 'high society'; *The Insider* negotiates a close friendship forged within oppressive institutional environments, in the publicly charged arena of politics, and in the notoriously protracted legal wrangling of 'Big Tobacco'. *The Straight Story* explores one man's personal journey to his brother over many months and miles; while *The Bridges of Madison County* holds attention on a four-day love affair, it is always alert to the long-lasting resonance of the encounter over a lifetime. While the first two films are more obviously grand in their designs – *The Age of Innocence* as richly ornate period drama; *The Insider* as 'big city thriller' – the latter two open up under (and reward) sustained scrutiny of their intricacy and expansiveness.

Exploring intimacy and/as style

While intimacy is occasionally alluded to in Film Studies, it has been overlooked as a connective aspect of mise-en-scène. More often than not, intimacy is addressed as a quality of engagement between viewer and character (we are offered many intimate portraits of figures in film; we may also feel an intimate bond with a particular protagonist).[2] Equally, it might be raised as a marker of specific genres' story conventions, such as the humorously rocky road to love in a romantic comedy, the sexual intimacy of a steamy love affair in a raunchy thriller, or as marking out the overwrought passions of a melodrama. (Indeed, the different genres of the four films nurture heightened emotional registers: the paranoid thriller, family sagas, journey films, homespun melodramas. All four are aware of their bloodlines, yet find nuance in bold tones.) The following readings remain alert to the manner in which a particular film may seek to locate our feelings alongside those of a character in specific ways, and how narrative conventions lead to particular opportunities for distinct registers of intimacy. They differ from prevailing approaches to the subject by considering intimacy as a pivotal agent of film style.

The measures and expressions of intimacy are distinct in each film, and stem from differently arranged relationships of style and structure. Rather than considering the films as adaptations of literary material (as is most often the case with the chosen four),[3] as works of a particular genre, or as part of the directors' *oeuvres*, this book looks instead at their comparative stylistic arrangements, focusing on camera placement and editing technique, setting and composition, performance and gesture. The book is structured so that each chapter considers the films' individual handling of a shared element of film style. Chapter 1 introduces thoughts on place and patterning, considering the way some of the films shape their landscapes to achieve complex levels of integration between character and setting. Chapter 2 engages with patterns and punctuations of gesture. It shows how the use of gesture is a good example of how the films discriminate differently in their expressions of intimacy. In *The Age of Innocence*, publicly pronounced and performed gestures are composed to conceal personal meanings. Contrastingly, the gestures in *The Bridges of Madison County* comprise a domestic micro-melodrama of movement and emotion. Chapter 3 attends to dialogue, as 'voice and conversation'. In concise examples (or 'fragments') from the films, the chapter details how a precise crafting of words gathers meaning across the body of a film, in garrulous moments and punctuations of silence. Chapter 4 continues the discussion of aural intricacy in the films, moving on to consider the musical elements of two of the works. Specifically, it notes the precise introduction, placement, and development of pieces of music, of repetition and variation, and the coupling of particular overarching themes. Chapter 5 concentrates on the employment of dissolves and ellipses to compress great spans of time, and to weight the significance of certain experiences and events. The sixth and final chapter returns and extends attention to location, this time focusing on position and perspective, on the *standpoint* of the films in relation to their characters. It examines how the relationship of camera and character comprises an authoritative channel of intimacy. A binding concern of the first and last chapters is that of 'the most dramatic stylistic entity': space (Farber 1971: 3). As Farber sets out in *Negative Space*, 'There are several types of movie space, the three most important being: (1) the field of the screen, (2) the psychological space of the actor, and (3) the area of experience and geography that the film covers' (1971: 3).

In the course of the book, some sequences are returned to from different positions, not only to draw attention to the intricacy and synthesis of style within the films, but also to provide an increasingly intimate view of the films' dynamics. The chosen points of focus and overarching approach also permit a comparative contemplation of films that would not normally be considered in relation to one another, and, in turn, for overlooked achievements of the films to be revealed and appreciated.

Style and interpretation

The overarching approach of this book is one of stylistic interpretation and evaluation; we might call this expressive criticism. It follows a methodological description by John Gibbs and Douglas Pye in *Style and Meaning: Studies in the Detailed Analysis of Film*:

> To understand style is to interpret what it does ... Every decision taken in making a film – where to place the camera, which lens to use, when to cut, how to place the actors in space, how to clothe them – is taken in a specific context, informed by powerful conventions but unique to this moment in this film. Each decision – made in relation to the multiple patterns being built up across the film – develops the narrative and thematic web. Every shot is a view of something, every cut is from one specific view to another, every costume decision bears on considerations of character, situation, fashion context, colour design, and more. Much filmmaking seems to encourage us to treat this complex tapestry of decision making as 'transparent', so that we are often unaware of the craft and artifice involved. But all this decision making is material and it has material effects on our experience of them.
>
> (2005: 10–11)

The remarks by Gibbs and Pye lead to thoughts by kindred writers and critics, equally essential to this book. While narrative cinema uses a set of conventional techniques of form and expression, the *particularity* of a film's handling of a point of style, as 'unique to this moment in this film', carries potential and individual meaning. For instance, in *Reading Hollywood: Spaces and Meanings in American Film*, Deborah Thomas calls attention to the meaning to be found in the choice and display of décor in *It's a Wonderful Life* (Frank Capra, 1946). The scene in question concerns Peter Bailey (Samuel S. Hinds) as he tries to persuade his son George (James Stewart) to come to work at the Bailey Building and Loan Company after his time at college. Thomas makes the following observations:

> The subtleties of the two actors' performances are worthy of our attention and make it difficult to detach ourselves sufficiently from the emotional focus of the scene to look around at the details of the domestic setting. However, if we manage to do so, we may notice two cases of mounted butterflies in frames on the wall in the background behind Peter Bailey. It may be presumed that the butterflies have been collected by George, since they make an appearance later in his marital home, a repetition which reinforces the sense of their importance, and one of their functions in the scene with George and his father is undoubtedly to enhance the homeliness of the setting and to indicate the pride that George's parents feel towards their sons. Nevertheless, in a film about an angel trying to earn his wings and in which George himself longs to travel and is continually frustrated in his desires – while having to show pride and conceal resentment at his younger brother's wartime success as a flier – it is certainly pertinent that the objects on the wall are butterflies rather than anything else ... This one small detail in the film's decor serves to unlock a number of issues relating to other scenes and characters than the ones at hand, while ranging over a number of important themes: freedom, filial duty, disappointment.
>
> (2001: 3)

To understand a point of style, an apparently irrelevant and non-prominent item of décor, Thomas offers an interpretation. A moment of choice allows the film to express 'key aspects of [its] thematic concerns by integrating such issues into the setting itself' (5). Thomas's interpretation also points up the significance that can be found when considering the repetition or patterning of certain visual details across shots, sequences, and the film as a whole. The relationship between different stylistic elements is equally revealing. To return to and extend Thomas's example, further meanings of the décor arise from considerations of the placement of the camera, and the positioning of the character:

> [T]he fact that the butterflies are visually linked to George's father more than to George himself through the composition of the

image which places the butterflies at Peter Bailey's back is also important ... [as he] increasingly reveals his own disappointment through the scene, encouraging George to do all he can to get away from Bedford Falls and realise his ambitions, rather than remaining and crawling to Potter (Lionel Barrymore) as he himself had to do.

(4)

It is the interaction of stylistic elements that creates a 'complex tapestry of decision making', and, in turn, significance in film. As V. F. Perkins pronounces in *Film as Film: Understanding and Judging Movies*, 'The specifically filmic qualities derive from the *complex*, not from any one of its components. What distinguishes film from other media, and the fiction movie from other forms, is none of the elements but their combination, interaction, fusion' (1993: 117).

Just as one is called upon to consider the interaction of a film's stylistic components, it is equally vital to attend to their complex and shifting relationship, as it develops moment to moment. As Perkins writes, again in *Film as Film*, 'In order to comprehend whole meanings, rather than those parts of meanings which are present in verbal synopsis or visual code, attention must be paid to the whole content of shot, sequence, and film' (79). A response of this kind is found in Thomas's interpretation of the butterflies in *It's a Wonderful Life*. One recalls the claim that, 'This one small detail in the film's décor *serves to unlock a number of issues relating to other scenes and characters than the one at hand*, while ranging over a number of important themes: freedom, filial duty, disappointment'. Attention to content from shot to shot, sequence to sequence also allows for a clearer consideration of the 'multiple patterns built up across the film' referred to in Gibbs and Pye's remarks. Thomas is alert to the meaning that can be accrued by visual patterning when she states, 'It may be presumed that the butterflies have been collected by George, since they make an appearance later in his marital home, *a repetition which reinforces the sense of their importance*.'

It is in the organisation of moments, the arrangements and relationships of style, and the patterning of details that a film creates meaning. In *Film Performance: from Achievement to Appreciation*, Andrew Klevan details the depth of integration that is achieved in certain films, and in certain moments of film. Treating 'performance as an internal element of style in synthesis with other aspects of film style', Klevan explores 'the achievement of expressive rapport' (2005: i). Considering a pivotal sequence in *The Scarlet Empress* (Josef von Sternberg, 1934) – in which a young Catherine the Great, formerly Sophia (Marlene Dietrich) transforms from a 'young flirtatious girl frolicking on the cusp of womanhood to the hardened Catherine the Great' (47) – Klevan provides the following passages of interpretative criticism:

> The integration of performer and environment effectively express changes in scale; Dietrich's body and costume are placed in relation to the surrounds to adjust her shape and size. Catherine seems squashed into the small stairway as she descends, still looking like a girl – rather like Alice after a potion, too big for the tiny doors and passageways of Wonderland – but one now growing to fill her surroundings. Her proximity to the walls is emphasised by her raised left arm, her palm patting the surface as she clip-clops down the steps. Her increasing intimacy with the décor, throughout the sequence, is intimately connected to her touching it; the tactility is potent, and here the image of Dietrich's hand and the sound of her feet draw out the textures.
>
> The crowning shot of the sequence soon follows, where Catherine matures before our eyes, transforming herself into the Scarlet Empress. The shot only lasts 15 seconds but it is economical and dense, one of the most richly achieved moments of transformation in cinema. It is a summation of the concerns of the sequence – shaping this soft woman and hardening her – and an occasion to view the performer in exquisite symbiosis with her environment. Performer and surrounds meld, and Dietrich is well *cast*. Catherine follows Count Alexei running up the stairs that she had only a moment ago descended. Her urgent ascent is viewed from the top of the stairs, and she gets ever closer, eventually enveloping the image: she runs headlong into a darkness that she herself creates. This is the point at which the film moves back inside the bedroom and the Count shuts the secret door. This grained wooden door fills the frame, and dissolves slightly, decreasing in prominence, to show Catherine standing behind. The wood is patterned with a 'V' shape, and the dissolve allows it to graphically match the 'V' of Catherine's dress, gluing the

images together, and tightening the superimposition. She seems to occupy exactly the same space as the door; a ghostly figure caught walking through a wall. She stares out, as if watching them, and because we are able to see her, through the solid door, it appears that she is able to see through it. She does in fact *see* even though she cannot see (into the room). Indeed, the door then evaporates completely, and as Catherine is left clear in the image, she is left to see a clear picture. Suddenly, she sees through everything.

(50–2)

The involvement of the writing centres on the involvement of points of style, in significant relationships. The first sentence announces an interest in the 'integration of performer and environment', a relationship that tightens with 'increasing intimacy', inspired by the proximity and tactility of character to décor. In these moments, in this film, the integration of stylistic elements is achieved at the deepest level. A sense of the tightness of the synthesis is evoked in the language used, as 'Performer and surrounds meld, and Dietrich is well *cast*', creating an 'exquisite symbiosis'. Considering the final moments of Catherine's transformation, Klevan sees the use of a dissolve heightening the effect of integration, 'gluing the images together, and tightening the superimposition'. As Catherine and her surroundings unify, so too do points of style and significance. While the performance of Dietrich, the form of the décor and the use of a dissolve are persuasively detailed as individually expressive, the profundity of the moment's meaning is seen to stem from the depth of stylistic integration.

At the same time, Klevan attends to the film's achievements in moment-by-moment shifts and developments, in the modulations that lead to the final point of calcification. While sustaining attention on two consecutive sequences, he considers the significance of their singularity, interrelation, and place in the film as a whole. The opening lines alert us to 'changes in scale', and relations of body and surroundings that 'adjust [Catherine's] shape and size'. The significance of each shot and sequence adheres to the relationship between them, in adjustments from one to the next. Catherine's transformation is *achieved* in the film's development, moment to moment. Klevan notes the film's variation of rhyming movements, up and down stairs. While Catherine goes down girlishly, 'squashed into the small stairway as she descends', she ascends to become Empress, 'running up the stairs that she had only a moment ago descended'. The rhyme of moments highlights the distinction between them, and thus emboldens Catherine's act of change. In between these two moments, Catherine's relationship with her environment is seen to develop gradually, shot to shot, as she grows closer to the surrounds, yielding to and absorbing their qualities of hardness. Finally, incremental development gives way to a moment of firm transformation. As 'a summation of the concerns of the sequence', the film's momentary movement through a dissolve is seen to allow for a shifting effect, with the meaning of the moment transforming alongside the Scarlet Empress: 'Suddenly, she sees through everything.' In a sensitive scrutiny of details, Klevan's evocative descriptions convey the film's achievements of stylistic integration, and the evolution of meaning.

The following readings showcase more modern films in which stylistic integration is also achieved at the deepest level, with meaning developing moment to moment. This tightness of synthesis is a form of intimacy in and of itself. This book is a close study of closeness. Intimacy is found in the close, significant relationships of style, and in the close, significant relationships between characters. Both are bound.

Appreciating the modern movie

The book brings to light a further relationship, between the critical approach employed and contemporary Hollywood cinema. Within the expressive tradition of film criticism, a sustained scrutiny of style and meaning is most usually associated with studies of classical Hollywood. This is perhaps best exemplified by the ongoing examination and appreciation of Max Ophuls's 1948 film *Letter from an Unknown Woman* in various journals and books.[4] This monograph on intimacy redirects the currents of the expressive tradition in contemplations of more modern American movies. A passage from Gibbs and Pye may be useful here, allegorically connecting linguistic form to the relationship between critic and film:

> As in conversation we constantly have to judge a speaker's relationship to the registers of the language she uses, so we have to

assess the film's relationship to its stylistic registers, the status decisions take on by virtue of their specific use in context.

(2005: 11)

If the rhetoric or stylistic register of contemporary films differs from that of the Golden Age, then our response, within a critical dialogue, may also require a reshaping of words with which to understand and judge the newer form. Contemporary Hollywood film speaks to us in a language that is related to the classicism of the Golden Age, but moves beyond it, branching out into distinct trajectories of stylistic relations. Adrian Martin calls for attention to be paid to this suggestion, and connects with thoughts on Perkins's position in *Film as Film*, in his article '*Mise en scène* is Dead, or The Expressive, The Excessive, The Technical, and The Stylish':

> In the relation of style to subject, of 'how' to 'what' – and this is, at base, what all arguments over *mise en scène* are about – Perkins favours a carefully built-up, somewhat unobtrusive stylistic rhetoric ... That is, the themes, ideas, events, situations, meanings, understandings, attitudes of the fiction are served and expressed by the stylistic strategies. This is – roughly – a definition of classicism in cinema; and, like all artistic forms, it posits a particular *economy* between the elements of style and subject. Is it true to say that contemporary – post-classical – American cinema is completely devoid of such an understanding of style?
>
> (1990: 2)

It is a rhetorical question about rhetoric. Martin continues by identifying three tiers of 'style–subject' relations in contemporary Hollywood cinema. Each tier is composed of works whose textual economy is classical, expressionist, or mannerist. Martin provides a series of 'shorthand equations' for the three groupings. Films working within a strategy of style in the classical sense operate such that 'modulations of stylistic devices ... are keyed closely to [their] dramatic shifts and thematic developments' (3). Expressionist works have a textual economy 'at the level of a broad fit between elements of style and elements of subject ... in which general strategies of colour coding, camera viewpoint, sound design and so on enhance or reinforce the general "feel" or meaning of the subject matter' (3).

Mannerist films are the sort 'in which style performs out on its own trajectories, no longer working unobtrusively at the behest of the fiction and its demands of meaningfulness' (3).

A consideration of Martin's terms allows for further refinements, via a test of these criteria against the stylistic rhetoric of my own chosen set of films.[5] In displaying intricate patterns of organisation and coherence, all four films appear to belong to the first grouping, as works in which stylistic devices are 'keyed closely to dramatic shifts and thematic developments'. Yet, this 'pairing' is made complex, as elements which may initially be perceived as 'broad fit' components – epic landscapes, expansive vistas, magnified sounds – are also 'keyed closely' to the dramatic concerns of the four films, shaped to form expressions of intimacy. So, when dealing in the particular (of a certain film, of a certain moment of film), more precise discriminations move us beyond the 'sliding scale' of Martin's groupings. In certain instances, the 'big architecture' of the films is shaped into meticulous patterns of composition, repetition, and variation. Equally, at points, there is a balance of grandeur of scale, and austerity of action. Other moments accrue significance from the way 'bold' stylistic statements are 'refined by the pattern of detail built over and around them' (Perkins 1993: 119). It is one of the aims of the following chapters to distinguish how the four films discriminate in this way.

Martin's tiers and definitions offer a crucial entry point, facilitating discussions of the relationship between the rhetoric of expressive or mise-en-scène criticism, and that of classical and contemporary Hollywood film. The book seeks to continue, and to continue to refine, the vocabulary of sustained criticism of modern movies. In his response to Gibbs's book *Mise-en-Scène: Film Style and Interpretation*, Martin raises the point that 'it is not hard to form the impression of a critical practice still lolling in the sophisticated pleasures of *The Philadelphia Story* and *Touch of Evil*, and not moving much beyond that golden age of Hollywood classicism at its most refined and complex' (2004: 4). Alongside Martin, there are a small number of critics who have 'lolled' in the 'sophisticated pleasures' of the Golden Age *and* turned their attention to contemporary Hollywood.[6] In opening up thoughts on a particular pattern of significance and modulation of scale (or, to use Martin's words, a 'particular economy of style and subject'), I hope to be contributing another aspect to this body of writing.

Film Studies and contemporary Hollywood

A further reason why academia has on the whole resisted interpretative criticism of modern Hollywood is that the attention of Film Studies, in the 1990s, moved elsewhere. Gibbs and Pye raise awareness of this factor in the Introduction to *Style and Meaning*:

> In an era dubbed 'Post Theory' by David Bordwell and Noel Carroll – the title of their 1996 edited collection – the average university student will encounter a wide range of ways of engaging with the subject ... As a counter to what he identifies as the top-down approaches of subject-position theory and culturalism which proved so influential in the Film Studies of the last thirty years, Bordwell draws attention to another, more diverse trend in recent film scholarship. What he calls 'middle-level' research includes 'new film history', which has deepened our understanding of, among other topics, early cinema, non-Western national cinemas, industry practices, film reception and the history of film style; it also embraces work on film narrative, genre and point of view, as well as accounts of spectatorship which challenge the models presented by Theory ... An important but, on the face of it, curious feature of Bordwell's account – given the significance of film style within the field he describes – is the exclusion of interpretation.
>
> (2005: 1–2)

Predominantly, studies of contemporary Hollywood tend towards considerations of the broad over the particular. To borrow from the collective headings of *Contemporary Hollywood Cinema* (edited by Steve Neale and Murray Smith), from the 1990s onwards there have been five principal strands of study in this area. First (and perhaps as a binding concern), Film Studies consider the historiography of modern Hollywood.[7] Second, and echoing my opening comments, many scholars consider the economic situation of contemporary American cinema. In particular, aspects of globalisation and of the industry's business practices are examined in terms of their effect on the films produced.[8] Third, forms of technology used in Hollywood film are considered.[9] Fourth (and as a collation of distinct approaches sharing a focal point), the audience of contemporary American cinema is explored.[10] Fifth and last, there is a marked tendency to see the output of contemporary Hollywood as symptomatic of socio-cultural concerns.[11]

Of this latter grouping, when a concentration on an individual film does occur, it is often rendered as a 'case study'. In such instances, a theoretical framework is used to 'map' the 'text', so as to 'decode' its meanings. In particular, there is considerable interest in applying this process to analyse sexual and racial difference in contemporary popular films, to uncover underlying power structures. Two indicative passages are cited below. The first comes from an essay by Jude Davies and Carol R. Smith, entitled '*Wall Street*: Good Capitalism and Bad – The All-Male Family vs. Homosexual Seduction', the second from 'Tell the Right Story: Spike Lee and the Politics of Representative Style' by Sharon Willis. Willis discusses the position of two characters in Lee's *Jungle Fever* (1991). Both quotations follow together to allow for easy comparison:

> *Wall Street* figures capitalism through the relationship of three white males ... In screening what the film presents as different types of capitalism, the struggles over paternity in *Wall Street* act as a kind of master-code, displacing and domesticating its critique of Reaganomics ... Behind the screens of paternity, then, male homosexuality appears as the master-code underlying the film's disgust at Gekko's moral corruption, so that good and bad capitalism are encoded less by contesting affiliations between good and bad fathers, than by the conflict between allegiance to good father and to (male) seducer.
>
> (Davies and Smith 1997: 27)

> In a dominant cultural field that privileges visibility, that struggles with anxieties about the non-coincidence of the visible and the essential, *Jungle Fever* seems to play as much with the question of how people *look* – in both senses of the word – as it does with a discursive war of positions about the meaning of race and miscegenation. If Flipper and Angie are ciphers, their status as such is visually inscribed. More looked at than *looking*, their individual points of view are gradually submerged in the figure they make together that is the object of other people's looks ... Once they are coupled in a two-shot ... these characters rarely support point-of-view shots

that would allow our gaze to coincide with theirs. This is the cinematic mechanism that evacuates their interiority, but it also puts us in a position to observe how they function as signs that the other characters continually interpret.

(Willis 1997: 168–9)

While the writers are 'mapping the text' to discover what is 'really going on', and 'decoding' the 'ciphers' and 'signs', little attention is paid to the shifts and developments in the film's meanings, moment to moment.

One recent high-profile title which appears to set matters straight is David Bordwell's *The Way Hollywood Tells It: Story and Style in Modern Movies*. A consideration of this book and its approach points up certain tendencies and evasions in such discussions of modern American cinematic style. At first, *The Way Hollywood Tells It* seems set to address some similar concerns to my book, concentrating on readings about 'the art and craft' of contemporary Hollywood cinema: 'I want to tease apart the finished films and see what strategies of plot and visual style govern their design' (2006: 1, 17). Bordwell traces the historical continuity and development of different points of style in American cinema, from classical to contemporary periods. Written from a formalist perspective, his book documents the appearance of traditionally established stylistic elements in modern film without offering interpretative analysis. Bordwell lists films and moments of film as evidence of wider trends and tendencies, rather than as indicative of a particular film's excellence or expressive capabilities. The approach leads to collective considerations of technical features of filmmaking (such as lens length); in turn, despite the asserted intention to 'tease apart the finished films', a concentration on collective impulses leads away from a sustained analysis of individual works.

For instance, Bordwell's answer to his own question, 'Why are movies cut faster now?' comprises a listing of the ASL (average shot length) of over 50 films named in passing: '*The Crow* (1994), *U-Turn* (1997), and *Sleepy Hollow* (1999) come in at 2.7 seconds; *El Mariachi* (1992); *Armageddon* (1998), and *South Park* (1999) at 2.3 seconds. By century's end, the ASL of a typical film in any genre would run 3 to 6 seconds' (122). These flitting examples are presented without further analysis, and without enquiry into why this film cuts at this speed,

the effect, or the relationship between this decision and those involving other points of style. Instead, the collective information leads to
the broad observation that 'Intensified continuity can be traced in
large part to changes in production demands (such as shooting on
location, planning for the TV format, accelerating filming schedules),
craft practices (particularly multiple-camera shooting), and technical
tools (such as the Steadicam and digital editing)' (156–7). The encyclopaedic compilation of technical data and 'craft norms' subsumes
the individual films, and leads away from discussions of particularity
or meaning (such work is summarily dismissed by Bordwell as 'roundabout interpretations' [120]). This is despite a stated goal to address
how 'distinctive strategies' of style 'affect ... experience' (120).

When *The Way Hollywood Tells It* provides an example of 'close
analysis' (nine pages on *Jerry Maguire*, for instance), potentially
illuminating avenues of enquiry on the relationship between structure, style, and character (and, indeed in this case, on intimacy) are
quickly closed down by broad assertions, each dealt with in a single
short paragraph: 'Here the central character grows in self-knowledge';
'The film reworks the familiar duality of love versus money in
fairly complex ways'; 'As in the studio era, people are characterized
through facial expression and movement'. In turn, each point of
story and style is swiftly appraised in order to show that 'The deft
economy of *Jerry Maguire* is wholly grounded in the precepts of
orthodox filmmaking' (64–71).

In other instances, practitioners of Film Studies declare the desire
to move away from both the binary discoveries of decoding, and
encyclopaedic compilations, to hold attention on specific moments
of a film. An example of this type of writing is found in John Orr's
book, *Contemporary Cinema*. In a review of Orr's book, Tico Romao
describes the work as comprising 'close interpretations', and 'examples of evaluative criticism' (1999: 1, 5). The following three passages
are extracted from Chapter 6 of *Contemporary Cinema*, in which Orr
considers the film *Wild at Heart* (David Lynch, 1990):

> In *Wild at Heart*, the landscapes of the American South-West with
> its harsher light define the journey from the lushness of the old
> South into ochre desert landscapes. The photography of Frederick
> Elmes with its saturated reds and yellows stresses the pitiless
> heat and luminous summer light, offset by the deep blacks of

the nightscapes in New Orleans and the open road during the crashed car sequence. In the motel scene where Bobby Peru (Willem Defoe) threatens to rape Lula, the burnt gold feel of the interiors is a match to the exterior hues of a parched landscape. The local feel of the American South-West means we are patently somewhere, but we also feel we could be anywhere. The place has a name but no nature. It is a non-place on the road to unknown destiny.

(Orr 1998: 167)

The film is a 1990s version of *Love Me Tender*, where tenderness is the restful aftermath of lust, not its sentimental prelude. Yet though Lynch is symphonic, his narrative rests ... on disconnection. Flashback, ellipsis, continuity cuts and parallel montage offer the audience the chance to go with the metaphor of the road, a rapid-gear changing scenario to contrast with the actuality of the smooth convertible in which they drive.

(168)

Lynch's film shows that while [Fredric] Jameson's 'postmodern' is misplaced, his view of American conspiracy as the quest for an unreachable totality is unerringly right.

(168)

The first passage promises sustained attention on specific moments of *Wild at Heart*. Orr chooses to concentrate on particular aspects of style, on landscape and colour. His descriptions are atmospheric, detailing the 'ochre desert landscapes', and the 'deep blacks of the nightscapes'. In drawing attention to the 'ochre' of the land, and 'deep blacks', Orr is responding to a possibility of contemporary cinema. In modern film, intense textures of colour, sound and visual effect are made possible by advanced technological allowance. Adrian Martin considers the possibilities and intensities of these features in his 2000 article 'Delirious Enchantment'. Focusing on modern film, Martin describes the textural magnificence that is achieved by certain works, in moments of 'fine grain aesthetic control' (2000). In considering expressions and achievements of magnificent intimacy, this book also brings out textural details made possible by the new sound and image capacities of modern film. It explores aspects of amplification and refinement both visual and aural, such as the opalescent shimmer of light-beams in the closing moments of *The Age of Innocence*, the patterns of greens in the fields of *The Straight Story*, and the deep crunch of tyres in gravel in *The Bridges of Madison County*. Marking a distinction with the technical limits of earlier films of significance, these properties contribute to the expressive achievements of modern cinema.

Although Orr offers thoughts on individual moments in a film, emphasising the use of colour, his remarks, like Bordwell's (though in a different register), move increasingly away from the particular towards the broad. In the final lines of the first passage, vague condensations take the place of precise discriminations: 'The place has a name but no nature. It is a non-place on the road to unknown destiny.' The second and third passages evade close considerations of the film. A list of stylistic techniques – 'Flashback, ellipsis, continuity cuts and parallel montage' – takes the place of detailed scrutiny of the distribution, emphasis and significance of these effects in moments of film. The act of quickly herding points of style together captures the sense of speed expressed by the film. Yet it remains unclear how a flashback or the other effects convey a particular aspect of travel (in this moment, in this film). In turn, the precise nature of the 'metaphor of the road' remains hidden. The third passage reveals the piece to be ultimately locating *Wild at Heart* as a case study for grander designs (and a search for 'rights' and 'wrongs'), as Lynch's film 'shows that ... Jameson's "post-modern" is misplaced'. Orr provides valuable evocations of a general atmosphere, but does not interpret the chosen moments of film as described by Romao, other than to test the findings against theoretical models.

As indicative pieces of academic writing on style in contemporary Hollywood cinema, the work by Bordwell and Orr illustrates some prevalent evasions and elisions. There is a small number of writers dealing in the specifics, whose work informs the direction of the following chapters. These writers offer sustained interpretations on moments in modern American film. In devoting attention to the particular handling and consequences of a film's style, they yield evocative and sensitive observations. Their writings are *involved* in the expressive possibilities of contemporary Hollywood cinema. Considering *Unforgiven* (Clint Eastwood, 1992), Ed Gallafent details a moment in which a trail-hand offers a pony in recompense for his partner's earlier disfigurement of a local prostitute:

> This is an important moment in *Unforgiven*, expressive of the limit to which a plea for forgiveness can be taken, of how far the social order which we are seeing here is capable of change. The tempo of the sequence slows in a series of close-ups as the whores consider the possibility of a world based on impulses other than bodily urges and property rights – a gesture expressive of the difficulty of this moment is when one young woman lifts a muddied hand to her brow. But the offer is doomed – behind the young trail-hand is an unlikely but appropriate sign – its message reads 'Meat Market'. It is Strawberry Alice who speaks in furious rejection of the gift, and again – now Delilah and another girl are exceptions – the whores throw dirt at the retreating cowhand … The importance of the sequence is that it expresses the paradox at the heart of the presentation of Big Whiskey, a place in which it seems that a movement away from a degraded and barbarous order cannot actually be achieved, but where the possibility of something better is persistently sensed, and felt to be perhaps only just out of reach.
>
> (1994: 219)

Gallafent demonstrates his claim for the importance of the moment through the detailing of its synthetic qualities. To focus on one aspect of the interpretation, the significance of a single gesture is noted, 'when one young woman lifts a muddied hand to her brow'. The interpretation sees the gesture as encapsulating both the tension and complexity of the moment. We can picture the movement of hand to brow, and sense the ambivalence held within it: a gesture at once impulsive and measured, outwardly demonstrative yet defensive, ready to grab yet restrained, dignified but, in this instance, 'muddied'. The movement and the moment are seen as expressing a paradox, the little gesture detailing the wider representation of a place 'where the possibility of somewhere better is persistently sensed, and felt to be perhaps only just out of reach'. The interpretation is sensitive to the film's own sensitivity, of holding these matters in suspension, as delicately poised as the hand to the brow. 'Honing in on moments', as Klevan notes, 'is a method of magnification'

(Gibbs and Pye 2005: 215). He continues, 'We can survey the inter-weaving contours of the drama and better discern the undulating lines without needing to straighten them out' (ibid.). In this way Gallafent's interpretation, rather than trying to 'solve' the film by analysis, is 'responsive to the overlaps, [keeping] in play the balance of meanings' (ibid.).

A passage of Klevan's own writing on contemporary Hollywood emphasises how concentration on a moment may open up a better understanding of the film as a whole. Again, a seemingly minor gesture captures a wider concern. Writing about *Titanic* (James Cameron, 1997), Klevan is also alert to notions of *balance*:

> In a film of much flooding, and falling, and flailing, it is pleasing that the film's most potent moment, or at least for its protagonist Rose (Kate Winslet), is a sight of human stillness, a posture of bodily poise necessitated by upper class manners. Rose looks across the extravagant dining hall and sees a young girl with her family. The camera then indicates Rose's particular attention: the young girl is making the effort to position her legs *correctly* so as to allow her napkin to remain tidily and safely perched upon her lap. Class rules often convincingly masquerade as essential practicalities, but this picture of precious suspension permits Rose a moment of lucidity, where she comprehends a young girl's social and parental education, and hence her own, both in terms of straining towards contrived balance, and keeping one's legs together ... Thus the ship's massive break-up services Rose's own desire to break out, a dream of wild release, expressed in the form of a recurring nightmare for the upper classes, where a world of people obsessed with bodily composure endlessly slide and slide – unlike the napkin – down and down the deck.
>
> (1998: 307–8)

The passage brings together, and highlights the integration of, distinct elements of style. In doing so, it details the film's graded measures of assertion and delicacy contained in a single scene: the grand setting of the 'extravagant dining hall', the little trapping of the napkin, the carefully considered gesture. Chiming with Gallafent's piece, this single gesture carries aspects of significance that are patterned throughout the film. The delicate poise of the napkin carries the weight, in pocketed form, of the 'contrived balance' of the upended boat towards the end of the film. The interpretation also reveals further aspects of poise and balance found within the film: of human stillness against frenzied movement, of control and containment against 'wild release'. Again, a passage of writing opens an understanding of the film through sensitivity to its suspensions. There is another grade of significance here. To capture the expressive form of this disaster-movie's moments, Klevan uses words loaded with life. To cite his own phrasing from another piece, especially apt for a watery work such as *Titanic*, Klevan shapes the interpretation with words in the 'stream and flow of the film' (Gibbs and Pye 2005: 224). Consider again the opening lines:

> In a film of much flooding, and falling, and flailing, it is pleasing that the film's most potent moment, or at least for its protagonist Rose (Kate Winslet), is a sight of human stillness, a posture of bodily poise necessitated by upper class manners.

The immediate repetition of 'f', with the flatness of the sound gliding the words together, captures the fates of the passengers of the Titanic, as they 'endlessly slide and slide ... down and down the deck'. These last lines re-emphasise the effect. The repeated, elongated vowel sound of 'down' conveys stretches of sustained motion; the change to the more abrupt and harshly clipped 'deck' sounds the grim end of the fall. Correspondingly, the slide of 'flooding, and falling, and flailing' is brought to a stop by the repeated 'p' of 'pleasing', 'protagonist', 'potent', 'posture', and 'poise'. The pert 'p' stands in counterpoint to the flat 'f', carrying the way the controlled position of the young girl's legs and napkin contrasts with the shifting havoc of the shipwreck. The prim sound of the repeated 'p' also expresses the 'just-so' precision of the girl's efforts. Action and words are *composed*. The use of language adds another level of interpretative evocation to the writing, in turn heightening our understanding of the particular achievements of the film. The words are precisely chosen to meet the stylistic register of *Titanic*, pointing up the delicate weighting in a huge film preoccupied with matters of size and scale.

But what does it tell us about contemporary Hollywood?

  The following chapters seek to hold true to the principles guiding the above passages of interpretative criticism. Rather than 'mapping the territory' in any grand sense or scheme, this book makes claims for patterns of organisation and synthesis in certain contemporary Hollywood films as precisely and particularly expressive of the works' individual achievements on a shared theme: the bond of stylistic and human relationships. Instead of a broad cataloguing of the appearance of dominant stylistic strategies, *Hollywood and Intimacy* offers, in the pursuit of persuasive evaluation, a better understanding of the fine-grain discernments within the films themselves.

•••

The inflatedness of contemporary Hollywood cinema allows for particular patterns of expression. It is an overlooked possibility of the modern movie, as shown in the four films under scrutiny, to shape potentially 'bloated' components into fine arrangements of significance. The handling of points of style, and stylistic relationships, that comprise the 'big architecture' of a film, allow for articulations of intimacy. This book continues a tradition of expressive criticism, and redirects some of the approach's principles, making claims for discernible patterns of organisation and synthesis in Hollywood film of the 1990s. Against certain highlighted tendencies and evasions of 'Post-Theory' Film Studies, the book offers another way of considering and appreciating contemporary Hollywood. The following interpretations join the contributions of a small and growing number of critics, seeking to understand and elucidate some of the rhetorical features of modern American cinema.

1
Place and Patterning

The Straight Story

Movements across the landscape

Elderly Alvin Straight (Richard Farnsworth) makes the big decision to travel more than 300 miles to visit his ailing brother Lyle (Harry Dean Stanton). Due to his own deteriorating health, Alvin is unable to drive a car; doggedly, he determines to make the trek by the unusual and time-consuming method of riding a sit-on lawnmower across country. The great distance in miles is met by the extent of the men's emotional separation, of the 30 years they have chosen to remain apart. As the film focuses on Alvin's travels from Laurens, Iowa to Mount Zion, Wisconsin, it presents a journey of immense personal importance over the awesome terrains of the American Midwest. Certain critics have alluded to the film's handling of matters of magnitude within one man's personal odyssey. Stanley Kauffmann proclaims that 'Lynch has made a small epic' (1999: 28). Rather opaquely (though beautifully), Wesley Morris sees *The Straight Story* as 'A journey film kissed by tiny magic' (1999). Both remarks touch upon a key relationship in the film, of grand-scale matters (the 'epic' nature of this 'journey film') measured out in diminutive detail (the 'small' and 'tiny magic'). This chapter explores the intricate facets of this relationship at work, of a significant journey formed through an accrual of illuminating moments.

Charting the length of Alvin's vast journey, *The Straight Story* frequently moves to sweeping long shots of the natural landscape. With the breadth of a bird's eye view, the camera glides over lines of trees, crop fields, and hillsides. Held across the widescreen expanse, these imposing Midwest vistas convey the scope and weight of the pilgrimage. By degrees, the film develops this relationship beyond a simple tallying of distance. It pays attention to the way natural details alter the overall shape of the land. It avoids leaden or reductive expressions (of a burdensome voyage over vast countryside) by picking out particular landscape features *in relief*. A good example comes in the camera's repeated tracking of the geometrical arrangements of croplines. Passing over thick rows of tawny reeds, it shows how some stalks and branches bend in naturally warped uniformity. In alternating its focus between such intricacies of the land and Alvin's movement forwards, the film suggests how the rural arrangements reflect the ordered composure of the character's travels. Progressive unbroken curves of wheat and grass rhyme with Alvin's smooth unruffled turns along the road. Far from conveying the daunting nature of a grand space and task, the film uses long landscape shots to suggest the tempered fluency of Alvin's pastoral progress.

The film refines the connection, shaping its treatment of the landscape to capture the protagonist's passing moods. Lines of the land follow shifts and turns in Alvin's attitude towards his journey. Two instances show how the film's movements across the landscape express exact feelings of pleasure and disquiet. In the first, Alvin deviates temporarily from the highway to shelter from an encroaching storm. As the rain drives down, the lawnmower draws under the frame of an empty barn, on top of a hillock by the roadside. Alvin sets himself towards the task of waiting out the weather. When the rain dries up, the changing aspect of the land expresses Alvin's refreshed approach. Angling up from the tattered barn, the camera cuts through sunshine to show a landscape charged with a sense of restoration. Appearing grey and dour during the rainfall, the terrain is once again infused with bright greens and yellows, as light dapples the smooth swell of the hills. The leisurely movement of the lens, forwards and from side to side, gracefully traces out the flowing warp and weft of field and way. A satisfying fusion of colour, texture, and movement suggests the pleasure to be taken in this passage.

Alongside appreciative views of journeying, the film occasionally presents brief instances of toil. The second example hints at passing sensations of strain within a continuous movement onwards. Just prior to Alvin's on-road encounter with a group of passing cyclists, a dissolve bleeds together a close image of the mower and a long shot of the landscape. The mower is shown travelling slowly along the horizontal axis of the road. As the views merge, this right-to-left movement is held in tension with an upward track along vertical columns of wheat. In the blended images, Alvin moves across the crops, *against the grain* (see Figure 1.1). Crucially, this crossing only endures within the space of the dissolve. The suggestion of modestly laboured movement passes as a twinge.

Alert to the nature of rural terrain, *The Straight Story* pays equal attention to the pervasive feature of the road. Like the surrounding fields and hills, the film explores the intricacies of the road through Alvin's presence. As with the wider landscape, the sight of a boundless track is in turn refined, and individually inflected. As a monumental icon, 'The Road' carries with it a weighty set of associations. The distinctly American film genre of the road movie – from *Easy Rider* (Dennis Hopper, 1969) and *Two-Lane Blacktop* (Monte Hellman, 1971) to *Rain Man* (Barry Levinson, 1988) and Lynch's own *Lost Highway* (1997) – carries a rich collective history of visual tropes, stylistic markers, and thematic potentiality. Beyond film, the road marks many forms of American art. Discussing the photographic work of Robert Frank, Jay Tobler describes 'the American highway stretching endlessly into the distance' as 'a potential symbol of freedom, endless

Figure 1.1   *The Straight Story* (David Lynch, 1999): Alvin goes against the grain

promise, and possibility' (2001: 151). At the same time, he sees the road as capable of suggesting 'the alienating effects of a vast, unbroken emptiness, the anxiety of the traveller with too far to go and too little gas' (151). *The Straight Story* draws on and reorganises many markers of the road movie; at the same time, it combines Tobler's understandings, though in measured, personal forms. The film uses a repetition of long shots to express the 'endless' nature of this constant dusty yellow line, tracing its tracks over the hills. The long shots capture the 'unbroken' nature of the road, leading Alvin to his brother. It is shown as a connecting thread, offering a continual reminder of the 'possibility' of reconciliation with Lyle.

The film's use of extreme long shots may at first be seen to stress the 'anxiety' created in Alvin by the scope of his journey. The high shots show a tiny vehicle on a vast strip, as if a fly on flypaper. However, in coupling the wide views with optical point of view and reaction shots, the film alters this sensation, instead creating expressions of favourable dependency. In a combination of perspectives, the film conveys how Alvin enjoys his position, placing faith in the road, taking pleasure in its features (to be addressed in more detail in Chapter 6). It uses a recurrence of tight optical point-of-view shots of the road's surface from Alvin's perspective. Instantly, the shots emphasise the physical proximity of traveller and road. Through these views, the film focuses on the slow rhythmic passage of dashed road markings. The al fresco, dawdling mode of the mower affords Alvin a greater sense of involvement with his surroundings. Without the restrictive casings of a car, Alvin can peer down to scrutinise the textures and surfaces of the road. A slow pace allows for a longer study. Like the natural landscape, the road can also carry signs of Alvin's demeanour. A sense of steady resolve is felt as the track is etched out in equal dashes. Along with a regular pace, the smooth and uniform flow of marked lines suggests how one brother's persistence to go the distance and reach the other remains evenly measured.

As well as examining features of the highway itself, the film pays equal attention to the mower's position on the road. The film gradually increases the bind between traveller and terrain by moving through views of Alvin on the road in a particular order. The order can be traced through in the analysis, moving from wide views of the mower on the track, into corresponding close shots. In repeated long shot, Alvin is shown driving tight to the side of the highway, taking up little space on the strip. His position underlines his humble standpoint. He accepts a situation suited to his gradual progress, yielding the main part of the road to the speedier passage of cars and trucks. Crucially, in this position, the wheels of the mower are seen to straddle the road and the verging grassland. From the all-encompassing distance of a long shot, the position of the wheels creates a tangible bond between the mower and the landscape. The mower's straddling of two distinct spaces, of road and field, succeeds in giving both aspects equal weight. Simultaneously, the position involves Alvin in both aspects of the immediate surround. Road and track support the mower; in turn, Alvin's rig acts as a supporting device for the different surfaces. It suspends the two planes, holding them in tension. As the film cuts to closer shots of the mower (and so to its wheels), the inference is developed even further. In close shot, the superimposition of a single wheel on the broad natural canvas inflects the appearance of both. The adjacency of two familiar sights in an unfamiliar coupling, of a mower and a rural highway, makes them strange. The wheel vivifies the views of the landscape, and vice versa.[1] Natural and synthetic textures meet in the arching presence of the mower.

The film is equally careful in its withdrawals of the camera from the mower, as with its approaches. At points, the film reduces the 'alienating effects' of a vast landscape by gradually disclosing its far-reaching views, moving from the mower outwards. To cite a striking example, this effect occurs as the mower passes a hitchhiker (Crystal, played by Anastasia Webb) waiting by the side of the road. Alvin's approach towards the girl opens with a close-up shot of the mower's wheel. Moving tightly across the body of the vehicle, the camera slowly pivots out, revealing the surroundings in a widening viewpoint. In the instance, the mower acts as a mainstay to the motion. The film introduces the greater vista by subtle degrees, while keeping tight to the vehicle. Rather than counter Alvin's diminutive position with the grandeur of 'Nature', the move allows the film to release views gently alongside him. In turn, the association between the individual man and the composite surroundings is made closer. In moving towards and away from the mower with equal measures of delicacy, the film individualises the vast tracks of road and field. Progressively, the broad canvas of the landscape is imbued with Alvin's presence.

Circles and straight lines

Alvin's journey is also measured in a series of concise circular moves, with the incremental development of these circles composing a 'Straight Story'. On the broadest level of narrative structure, the film charts Alvin's progress in a straight line. It adheres strictly to chronological, linear development. However, even on this level, the film creates circular moves. The most momentous instance occurs as Alvin's mower breaks down. Stranded on the road, Alvin makes the decision to return home and start the journey again. Yet, the film also presents circular moves that carry Alvin forwards. A repeated juxtaposition, of close shots of the mower's turning wheel with long shots of the road, conveys this idea in its simplest form. *The Straight Story* creates intricate designs by exploring the accrual of circular turns in greater depth. The mower's wheels can be seen as the starting point of the film's explorations: a lynchpin to which the film often returns in its circular views.

There are two distinct, though interrelated ways in which the film creates individual, circular patterns of Alvin's progress. First, circles are formed in the physical movements of the camera, in the turn of the lens over long shots of the terrain. The film carries smoothly across distinct locations by following a single continuous through-line of camera movement. Such fluid moves consist of a meticulously arranged series of circles and straight lines. Secondly, *The Straight Story* creates circles in its patterning of particular visual motifs. In Alvin's various meetings and encounters on the road, the film creates a series of miniature tales that appear self-contained, as complete in and of themselves. At the same time, the encounters are integral parts of the character's greater expedition. The film achieves this dual effect through the shaping of cyclic patterns of motifs. In camera movement and editing, *The Straight Story* presents a single journey unfurling through the passage and growth of compendious circles.

The opening sequence introduces an interest in circular arrangements and patterning. Slowly, the camera releases its gaze from a sky of stars to turn and sail over crop-fields, on into the town of Laurens, before settling in front of Alvin's yard. Through each turn, the film increasingly narrows its point of focus, moving from a myriad of stars to a single house. The effect hints at Alvin's own later trajectory, as he takes in the sweeping vistas offered by the countryside, before finally directing his focus, steering the mower down the narrow pathway to Lyle's lone shack. The opening sequence is alternately performed as a series of circular rotations and straight courses. First, the camera turns around the land. It then advances over consonant surfaces in straight lines. The order repeats before we approach the Straight yard. Two full turns and strokes of the land bridged by dissolves carry us to Alvin's house, from the stars. The film bleeds together textures and parallel lines through the dissolving shots: dots of light; waving wheat fields; long stretches of grass, roads, and street paths. The film's precise pattern of camera moves (circle, stroke), and its merger of textural details form a fine tapestry, dedicated to the processes of travelling. The opening moments knit together the film's overarching concerns: a short prelude to grander designs.

Such intricate views continue to chart Alvin's passage. In one good example, two consecutive legs of the journey are bound together into a single circle. Like the opening sequence, a bind is achieved through an exact match of parallel lines, formed within a circling turn, this time through big manmade structures. It occurs as the journey takes Alvin from road to bridge, just prior to his crossing of the Mississippi River. The film presents extreme long shots of settings, road, and bridge, and places them together in a circular move. First, the camera leads steadily away from multiple forks in a road junction to one horizontal strand of the track. From a bird's eye view, the road is shown as a thin grey line set atop swathes of grassland. In rotation, the road appears as a needle on a compass, moving to point north by northeast. As the line turns, a dissolve brings in a matching view of the bridge (see Figure 1.2). Both point in the same direction in the frame, and point the way for Alvin. Through the camera's tracing of a circle and the use of a dissolve, two monumental settings – the Midwest road and a bridge crossing the vast width of the Mississippi River – are linked as matching straight lines. As the single circle is sealed, the film suggests how each stage of the journey feeds perfectly into the next, as a series of intimately connected endeavours.

Passing encounters with people 'on the road' receive similar treatment. Each meeting appears complete, as if Alvin and his momentary companion(s) have fulfilled all and any promise of their time together. At the same time, as each encounter is essentially transitory, happening 'by the way' on an ongoing trip, they are also expressed as fragments of a much greater journey. Each meeting has its own sense of intimate fullness, and plays a role in Alvin's coming reunion with

Figure 1.2   *The Straight Story* (David Lynch, 1999): View from a bridge

his brother. Again, the film's development of circular patterns is fundamental to this dual effect. On the second day of travelling, Alvin passes Crystal the hitchhiker. In the evening, he meets her again. The meetings play out in a move from day to night to day, and in cyclical returns of rhyming views: of horizons, the sun, kindling, Alvin's face. Through dissolves and in matching colours, shapes and textures, the repeat views tightly cohere, appearing organically bound. There is a natural congruity to the progressive views of wood, sun, and fire. The movement of the sun charts the entire encounter with the hitchhiker, reminding us (and elderly Alvin) that time is short. Coupling shots of firewood form bookends to the sequence. Within the rhyme lies a little and important distinction. The opening shot is of a naturally scattered pile of wood, lying pell-mell on the ground. The final shot shows a neatly bound bundle of sticks, handcrafted and tied together.

Crystal has left without saying goodbye, but leaves the careful bundle as a gift to say thank you for Alvin listening to her personal worries. The move from a messy cluster of twigs to a neat parcel forms a little act of advancement, in the sense of 'moving on' as well as 'putting things in order'. Within one sequence, the film weaves together interlacing designs of like images. In the ordering of views, of dramatic sunsets and the minutiae of Alvin's journey, the significance of clustering images slowly spirals. In all of the above examples, the meanings of small complete cycles of experience feed into those of Alvin's grand pilgrimage.

The Bridges of Madison County

Frames and boxes

Like *The Straight Story*, *The Bridges of Madison County* is set in the rural heartland of North America, in the cornfields and brush-hills of Iowa. In both films, the views of the landscape are charged with meaning. Though equally sensitive to the features of the shared countryside setting, the films work in opposing ways. Whereas *The Straight Story* charts Alvin's progress across an ever-changing landscape, *The Bridges of Madison County* focuses on a small number of fixed locations. Lynch's film examines the act of journeying, concentrating on a sustained movement across the breadth of the landscape. In contrast, Eastwood's work holds attention on the characters' crossing and re-crossing of the same spaces over time. In the matching Iowan setting, a sense of exposure is replaced by that of containment.

An emphasis on containment is in keeping with the film's story. Living a life of quiet domestic suffocation, farmer's wife Francesca Johnson (Meryl Streep) is offered a means of escape in the guise of travelling photographer Robert Kincaid (Clint Eastwood). As her family leaves town for the State Fair, Francesca spends four days with Robert. The brief encounter ends when the family returns from the trip, and Francesca returns to her life of little, regularly repeated errands and duties. The affair is concealed from the family, only to be revealed many years later and after Francesca's death, as the (grown) children revisit the homestead.

As well as concentrating attention on a few fixed settings – the family home, the kitchen, the bridges of Madison County – the film devotes itself to the discovery and unfurling of the four-day affair. Rather than working on a grand linear scale (the long roads and journey of *The Straight Story*), the film achieves a sense of expansiveness through the density of its exploration. It contains the affair in a series of frames and boxes, and gradually unpacks the details with meticulous attention. Richard Combs draws together these concerns, noting how, 'This "simple" love story is two hours fifteen in the telling, mainly because the film sets up so many frames, spatial and temporal, around the love interest: comings and goings to the domestic scene, a farm; the discovery of the story by the next generation' (1996: 26). The children's unearthing of the affair in 'the present' allows the film to shuttle back and forth across time, just as the characters carry across the same spaces. The effect is both elaborate and adds density to the film's structure. The film's use of the framing device can be traced to the source novel (by Robert James Waller), and yet marks an improvement, as Combs notes:

> [C]onsider how carefully Eastwood and screenwriter Richard LaGravenese have built around the original novel. This is itself an elaborately buttressed fiction, beginning in self-conscious mode with the author 'looking at the blinking cursor on the computer screen before me' when 'the telephone rings', and Francesca's grown children appear with her story after her death in 1989. The affair (which happened in 1965) is then unfolded in the present tense, with various digressions to Francesca recollecting it in the future, through letters, diaries, and Robert's last bequest (he dies in 1982). All this to-ing and fro-ing is not so much self-conscious as just rather precious and slippery. But the filmmakers have turned it into solid dramatic boxing by creating a framing story out of the children's discovery of the affair through the letters, their shock and slowly dawning appreciation of what their mother found, then renounced for their sakes.
>
> (1996: 27)

As the 'dramatic boxing' of temporal tenses is met with spatial 'comings and goings', the film explores the delicate variations coming from repeated visits to the same places. Within the confines of the farm, under the bridges and nearby locations, and the frame of 'just four days', Robert, Francesca and the film create patterns of activity, short-lived routines that rise above the conventions of the housewife's habitual life.

Fixed positions and open possibilities

As *The Bridges of Madison County* holds its attention on a cluster of settings, it promotes a sense of their fixity and solidity. For Francesca, the rigid hold of the settings becomes, at turns, a point of grievance, reassurance, and resignation. As she laments to Robert in the dying moments of their affair, 'You get caught ... and you just stop, and stay steady ... you just stop so your children can move.' Initially, this sense of grounding is expressed in approaches towards the Johnson house. In the opening moment of the film, the camera holds on the family's rusty mailbox, as a silver truck rolls up the driveway in a spray of dust. Only when the truck draws adjacent to the mailbox does the camera arc, with the vehicle, towards the house. The mailbox acts as fulcrum and sentry, supporting the turn into the grounds of the family home. It marks the edge of the homestead, carrying news from afar to this fixed spot. The titles fade in; we have entered the film in the first of many movements by trucks towards and away from this house.

Combs notes the film's attention to the approaches of trucks, stating that, 'It takes three of these vehicles to carry us properly into the story, and the repeated coming and going, this patient crossing of space and time, is another way of setting up a framework, of making the narrative approaches, as it were, concrete' (1996: 27). The first truck brings Francesca's son Michael (Victor Slezak) back to the family home, to join his sister Carolyn (Annie Corley) in sorting out their mother's estate. The second carries the family away from Francesca in 1965, to go to the State Fair. The sense of strain being taken from Francesca in this moment is held in the heavy freight of the truck, lumbering with the cargo of the cattle-box up the drive. The third truck brings Robert Kincaid. In all three instances, the weight of the trucks is expressed in their bulky design and the sound of their movement. With the engine's deep thrum, the wheels crunch down on the grit of the track. In stressing the heaviness of these vehicles, and in patiently holding on their slow movements towards and away from the house, the film suggests how the track to the farm becomes engraved through time, scored through passage. The flat landscape, of Iowan fields and long straight tracks, is made dense, thickened by the act of arriving and departing from one setting. In turn, the grooves of passage to the house point up Francesca's sense of being stuck in one place.

As the mailbox marks the edge of the Johnson estate, the porch-front stands as a border to the house itself. The film declares its interest in this boundary space in the opening moments, moving directly from the long shot of Michael's approaching truck to a tight view of Carolyn and the family lawyer standing on the porch. As Carolyn watches the truck roll up, the porch is used as a promontory, offering a clear vantage point from which to view the surrounding landscape. It offers a space for discovery, of the arrival of visitors; it also allows one to be discovered, to be seen and found. Standing on the porch, the characters pause upon a threshold between two settings: the close security of the house and the open countryside. These intertwining aspects are explored in a series of moments, and through the character of Francesca, over the course of the film.

Initially, the aspect of discovery is addressed in the first view of Robert Kincaid, from the edge of the porch. As the photographer's truck approaches the house, Francesca stands on the porch completing a chore, beating dust from a rug against one of the vertical wooden supports. It is a gesture of everyday duty, allowing for a little release of pressure, in each swing and beat of the rug. It is crucial to note that the task is performed against the posts of the porch; these struts support the roof, and at points throughout the film, bear the weight of the characters' bodies and actions. Here, the pressure of the task is taken by the post; Francesca does not lash out against the hard structures of the house, but uses their density and strength to brace her action. The truck's approach distracts the housewife from her task, and the rug slips to the floor. Francesca makes tentative steps to the porch edge, smoothing down her dress, straightening her posture, readying herself for a meeting. The vantage point offered by the platform allows the character small advantages, of declaring her presence before the approaching visitor, and of using the act of waiting to prepare for the moment of arrival.

Here the film strongly evokes similar scenarios and concerns in *The Searchers* (John Ford, 1956). The earlier film is equally interested in the use of porches and in structures around gender; both works suggest how a male figure appears as if 'summoned up' by a housewife. Ford's film begins with a lone rider, Ethan Edwards (John Wayne) approaching his brother's homestead; it develops patterns around his arrivals and departures, and the effect on Martha Edwards (Dorothy Jordan) as housewife, tracking their physical negotiations. Ed Buscombe asks of the opening of that film:

> The question – What makes a man wander? – may be specific to Ethan. If so, the opening scenes provide an answer: there is no place for him at home. But perhaps the question is more generally addressed, to us all. Westerns are rarely about settled domestic life, so often about men on their own, on the move. They offer a fantasy of freedom, a dream of life untrammelled by ties of home or work or the other fences which society surrounds us with ... But

might not women also want, in a part of themselves, to break free from domesticity and its responsibilities …? Don't we all have dreams of leaving?

(2000: 12–13)

The Bridges of Madison County takes up this question in Francesca's draw towards Robert's wandering, and her inherent hesitancies.

The natural caution and formality observed in an initial meeting between two strangers, especially on remote farmland, is suggested in the film's camerawork. There is a stark quality to the film's dryly measured repetition of angles and medium shots: from Francesca on the porch to Robert's truck. At this point, the camera keeps the characters apart. Francesca is set in the middle of the frame, in between the porch struts, quite guarded. Eyeing the oncoming truck, she comes to lean on the last post of the porch. Francesca's position expresses not only the openness of the situation, but also her mindfulness of the unknown visitor. In moving tight to the post, the character aligns herself with the home, housewife to house. Her stance suggests a need to draw support from her surroundings in face of an unknown man: a reassuring claim of territory. A bind to the house offers a source of fortitude.[2] On stepping from the truck to ask for directions, in trying to get his bearings, Robert, too, yields to familiar structures, resting his arm on the bonnet. Both figures find useful positions to bolster a moment of uncertainty.

There is also a sense of shared watchfulness, as the camera offers twinned over-the-shoulder perspectives: first, held close to Francesca, looking down from the porch to Robert; then back up again from the photographer's vantage point. A growing concentration of curiosity is matched with medium shots of the observed stranger, stressing the initial lack of reciprocal closeness. Yet, as the couple begins to talk, the camera moves gradually nearer to both in equally paced cuts. The film and characters are careful not to push too quickly into closeness, though; the camera holds on a set of incrementally tighter medium shots; the porch stands between the characters; they are framed separately in alternating views. Within a large frame, from a position of polite distance, small gestures of loosening-up begin to appear. Robert declares he is lost. In response, Francesca shuffles once to alter her stance, lifting her arm to press closer to the post. With the knowledge that the visitor has called to ask for directions, the suspense of irresolution falls away. A recalibration of the moment is sensed as Francesca's shoulders drop a little: a gentle adjustment.

At the same time, Francesca's close acquaintance with her surroundings creates a fresh prospect with this new contact, of giving and receiving directions. The film explores a stimulation coming within a circumscribed scenario, achieved here through the handling of physical and conversational positions. As Robert asks for the whereabouts of Roseman Bridge, there is another little adjustment: Francesca's guarded friendliness gradually shifts into a more open willingness to help, to enter into the conversation's contract. Robert's continuing request for more details becomes an invitation to sustain the meeting. The film marks Francesca's acceptance in her movement off the porch; in a step onto the verge she becomes level with Robert. She describes a neighbouring farm with its 'big mean yellow dog', arching her hands into clawed paws. As Francesca climbs down, her responses become more fluid and playful.

Robert's questions court Francesca's engagement while seeming to work towards a conclusion. Yet, in drawing out directions to the bridge, the outcome of this brief encounter is held at bay. Francesca joins in with an invitation of her own, and a joke. She could show Robert the location of the bridge – 'I can take you or tell you; either way; it's up to you; I don't care' – instead of using the afternoon to 'split the atom'. The joke releases a little tension and develops the sense of play. A quip gracefully lightens the boldness of Francesca's offer to accompany the stranger. It marks the end of their first exchange as a gentle punch line, and softens the impact of their mutual decision to go to the bridge together.

First, though, Francesca must get her shoes. The line encapsulates the character's attitude towards her surroundings, while hinting at an underlying spirit. It marks the fixity of her position; as there is no need to leave the house, there is no need for shoes. At the same time, though, it suggests a pleasure in open appreciation of her environment, of feeling the soil beneath one's feet. At the close of the moment, a final gesture on the porch underlines the film's attention to this compact space. Heading back for shoes and turning to the porch, Francesca reaches for the post, pushing against it for support. With a bend of the knee and a tilting roll of her hips, Francesca lifts herself up onto the promontory. Again, as she leans against the strut, the house takes the weight of her action. This time, though, it is a determined movement *against* the home's fixed ballast, marking a spirited decision to accompany the photographer. Raised and separated from Robert on the platform of the porch, Francesca steals a glance back.

Two consecutive moments centring on the tight space of the porch capture the tentative freedoms of a fledging relationship. Both instances follow the pair's trip to Roseman Bridge and their impromptu dinner at the house. Worrying the easy charm of the evening, Robert asks Francesca if she wants to leave her husband. As the question unsettles the mood, Robert, quietly embarrassed, takes his leave. Watching him go, Francesca stands in the open doorway to the porch, resting her hands on the frame, arms braced. On first sight, the image may be considered as melodramatically assertive, pointing to Francesca's 'entrapment' in and by the familiar domain of the house (see Figure 1.3). The housewife stands by the *stay* of the doorframe. Such an understanding is reinforced by a declamatory clap of thunder on the soundtrack, on the cusp of Robert's departure. However, when placed in relation to earlier movements on and around the struts of the porch, Francesca's position is made complex. In an instant of uneasiness, the character is momentarily bolstered by the solid brace of the doorframe. As she wavers on the threshold (not knowing if she is coming or going), Francesca uses the frame

Figure 1.3 The Bridges of Madison County (Clint Eastwood, 1995): The *stay* of the house

to steady a hesitation. A cry to Robert is caught in her throat as the telephone rings; duty calls; she retreats inside the house.

The resonance of the first meeting lingers still, encouraging an exploratory change in Francesca's relationship with familiar settings. Following the stranger's departure and after gathering her thoughts, the housewife sits on the porch to read. A gentle restlessness is felt in the rhythmic pitch of her rocking chair, suggesting a quiet distraction from the words on the page. The intermediary space of the porch encourages the sense of uncommitted contemplation. Possibilities are in the air. Moving from the chair, the character crosses to the porch's edge, loosening her gown, letting the night breeze push and billow the cotton folds. Francesca uses the space of the porch to open herself to her surroundings in a particular way; the place is at once private and open. Standing on the brink, she allows the wind to tease at her hair and clothes. Yet, the draught carries insects that soon nip at Francesca's exposed body, causing her to cover up again, to return indoors. The spontaneous moment of stimulation and release is short-lived, hinting at the essence of the affair to come.

The significance of these moments reverberates in the film's final view of the porch. The four days have passed; Francesca has made the decision to stay with her family, rather than leave with Robert. A fade to black gives way to a long shot of the family truck, as it pulls up the driveway to the farmhouse. The moment echoes Robert's initial arrival in the same space. The half-rhyme points up tensions between the occasions, and emphasises the impact of Robert's sudden absence. A crunch of gravel on the track alerts Francesca to her family's arrival. She stands in the doorway to the porch, watching through the portico's gauze screen. The camera looks in, through the hazy mesh. The gauze gives the shot a grey pallor; the arrival of the family is first greeted in mute tones. Francesca edges towards the door; the thin veil of the screen offers a slight guard, standing between the empty retreat of the house and a transparent moment of greeting. Echoing her reaction to Robert's arrival, Francesca readies herself for the reception. Here, she pushes down the pain of Robert's departure, finding a smile to fit the occasion. Her position behind the screen expresses a need for concealment, a veiling of emotion. Moving onto the exposed platform of the porch, Francesca musters a little display of welcome, clapping her hands together. She leans on the post, this time in a performance of relaxed and happy relief.

The film hints at the true undercurrent of feeling in two views of the dusty track. In the first, it matches the angle of the family truck pulling to a stop with the earlier shot of Robert's arrival. The exactness of the rhyme evokes a powerful irony through comparison. In the second, a stolen glance to the open track by camera and character couples a sense of longing for Robert's return with a fleeting wish for flight. The family car blocks the way.

Particular trappings hold and measure the anxiously contained stress of the reception. The load of a suitcase accompanies each family member. Francesca's strained expression of joy is now weighted with the bulk and burden of baggage; after the pressure of a forced greeting come the encumbering accoutrements of daily duty (so much dirty laundry to unpack and to pack away). As the family troops towards Francesca, the film draws in a view of swing-chairs set on the lawn. The heaviness introduced with the cluster of cases is developed in the sight of the chairs, each with a seat hanging down, suspended by rods and ropes. Weight is met by a sense of tautness and tightness. The inference develops as the camera moves with the family to the house, across the porch. The shot's angle highlights the close constriction of the family, held between porch struts and door. Whereas the porch once seemed the perfect place to survey possibilities, to breathe in and toy with the night air, it now appears a narrow space, restricted and restricting, as a curb to passage. The aspect of tightness amplifies in the sound of the porch door being opened, its rusty springs rasping and stretching taut. Setting and sound combine to capture the tension of the moment, of Francesca's tightly coiled emotions. As the family packs into the house, the door snaps shut.

Movements inside the home

Within the house, in the film as a whole, emotional resonance gradually gathers around the kitchen. The film forms patterns in recurring views of the kitchen and in the characters' traffic across the linoleum floor. In turn, this domestic location is gently animated by a developing significance. A repetition of views and moves meets the routine rhythms of business conducted in this space, of the preparing and taking of food. As in many households, the kitchen becomes the family nucleus. The Johnsons gather here to eat, though not to speak. The first view of Francesca declares a close association with this domestic space; she stoops in plumes of steam over the stove, preparing the family's dinner. The film's repeated focus on the place, and of Francesca's prescribed position within it, reinforces the sense of the character's fixity. As all the actions of the household pivot around the kitchen, Francesca is held in place. Yet, there are also expressions of flexibility in order. Most of Francesca's time with Robert is spent in the kitchen, drinking iced tea, fixing meals, eating dinner, dancing. The space forms the heart of the affair; the kitchen as nucleus becomes a centre of growth for the housewife. Equally, the informality and familiarity of the location allow the couple the room to adjust in their new relationship, to try out different stances.[3]

The film expresses how the characters adapt to changing situations within the kitchen by exploring the plasticity of the setting. In each instance, the placement of camera and cut shifts the aspect of the space and of changing personal relationships. Three moments reveal how the room is differently handled to match its occupants' feelings. The first is set in the 'present', as Michael and Carolyn sit at the kitchen table to read their mother's revelatory letters. The camera fixes on the two figures hunkered tight to the Formica surface. The table acts as an axis to the few measured tilts and turns by the camera, following the succinct moves of the characters to the coffee pot and into their seats. The moves are awkwardly confined. The low angle and closeness of the shot present a compact space, filled with the clutter of kitchen utensils and cooking bric-a-brac crowded on surfaces and shelves. In emphasising a sense of restriction, the film opens up multiple meanings. First, it conveys a feeling that arises from a return to a childhood place. The setting and décor of the family kitchen, once so homely, appear to have shrunk. At the same time, the particular circumstances are equally constricting. The letter is an uncomfortable find, holding tight their attention. In turn, the children's opinions of their mother's epistolary confessions are, at first, firmly unyielding. Only when they gain a less restricted view of the surrounding circumstances do they loosen up.

The first view of Francesca at work in the kitchen hints at the housewife's routes through rigidity. Moving from her initial tight spot by the stove, Francesca crosses the room to turn up the radio; the camera tracks with her as if authorised by the character, taking her lead, moving left to right, from and to the cooking pan. The action of Francesca traversing the room discloses its limits; at the same time, the twinned moves of camera and character suggest how the housewife takes pleasure in controlling confined situations, finding the space to do so. The act of turning up the radio is a measured move, a trim adjustment to a circumscribed environment. Yet, such little flourishes fall short of changing the bigger picture. The swell of the music points up the emptiness of the setting. The notes of the aria fall into space like dabs of paint on a blank canvas. The sense of vacuity is declared in a cut, as the film reframes to a long view of the kitchen's bounds (see Figure 1.4). The declamatory nature of the cut meets the pronounced positioning of the kitchen table, squarely set in the middle of the room. Francesca's refined appreciation of the music is held in tension with the perfunctory starkness of the setting. Her calls for the family to come to the table for dinner are also, at first, met with a blank lack of acknowledgement. As husband, son and daughter finally gather around the table with a scrape of chairs on the tiled floor, and a clatter of cutlery on the Formica surface, space and scenario appear brittle and functional rather than airily convivial.

In contrast, the possibilities of the kitchen as a place for casual cordiality are brought out in Francesca's first meeting with Robert. Returning from photographing Roseman Bridge, she invites him to stay for dinner. To prevent his film-stock spoiling in the heat of the

Figure 1.4 The Bridges of Madison County (Clint Eastwood, 1995): The kitchen's bounds

evening, Robert places the boxes in the fridge. The gesture is one of necessity, but also marks Robert's immediate ease with the setting, finding a place for his belongings. It forms a counterpoint with a later gesture, as Francesca's busybody neighbour comes to call. Filling the kitchen with noisy bluster, the portly neighbour swings open the refrigerator, rootling out the contents. A previous careful gesture of protection becomes one of pushy intrusion and exploitation.

The act of making dinner in the kitchen becomes a shared pursuit for the new acquaintances, quickly established as a comfortable ritual. The meals are casual and yet charged with thoughtfulness. The food preparations allow for a common and neutral point of focus; Robert falls in step with Francesca's domestic tasks. The sense of easy accommodation, of placing the film-stock in the fridge and helping to chop vegetables, is developed in Robert's quiet move through the porch door, as he retrieves bottles of beer from the truck. In earlier moments, Francesca's son and husband stride through the same door, letting it swing and bang on the jamb. Readying herself for this customary jolt, Francesca arches her back. Uncharacteristically, her heedfulness is smoothed away as Robert gently shuts the door without a sound. The way Robert adapts with ease and consideration to the spaces of the house allows Francesca to take pleasure in the act of adjusting to his company. At the same time, an apparently casual brush of the shoulders, as Robert reaches across Francesca to pick up a handful of vegetables, causes a frisson.

The film sustains this complex combination of accommodation and stimulation in the changing aspect of the kitchen space, as the evening develops. A dissolve moves to a moment of giddy conversation after the meal, as Robert describes an encounter overseas with an overly amorous orangutan (a sly nod to Eastwood's simian buddy in *Every Which Way But Loose* – James Fargo, 1978 – perhaps?). The camera is positioned in the corner of the darkened dining room, looking through an alcove into the glow of the kitchen. The effect of the framing is multiple. First, the new position opens up the space seen within the frame, suggestive of borders being pushed back. Simultaneously, it pulls the characters together, as the alcove is seen to close in the space around them. The angle draws attention to the couple's proximity as they laugh and talk around the kitchen table. Further, the withdrawal of the camera, and encroachment of frames in space, creates a sense of intimacy as left with these two characters at this moment. Placing the camera at a distance, the film leaves the characters together, to adapt to this new position of closeness. At the same time, the contrast between the darkness of the empty dining room and the compact glow of the kitchen through the alcove highlights both the concentration and unfamiliarity of this mood of tipsy warmth, in this setting. Last, the sight of the vacant dining table offers a pre-echo of the couple's final, awkward dinner together; the film contains the end of the relationship within its beginning.

After the giddiness of Robert's story, camera and character settle in closer, around the kitchen table. The couple sit one next to the other now, instead of on opposite sides. The smoke from their cigarettes fills the close space; holding the cigarettes out, their hands, tantalisingly, almost touch. The closer positioning meets an increasing sense of confidence within the conversation. Francesca asks Robert whether he is ever lonely, 'loving everyone but no-one in particular'. As the conversation unfurls and Robert responds, the camera reframes, showing that the kitchen door remains open between them. There are tensions in the image. The position of the camera and door promotes the aspect of exposure sensed in the candour of the couple's discussion, yet it also divides the space between them. Equally, the open door hints at the possibility of retreat from the house by Francesca, alongside the risk of Robert's imminent withdrawal. Through the framing and features of the domestic setting, the film expresses a moment of cautiously increasing familiarity, gently removed from commitment.

The Insider

Impersonal spaces and neutral locations

If, as Adam Phillips declares, 'intimacy is privileged information' (2000: 40), then a significant achievement of *The Insider* is its handling of the way two men forge a close relationship around a concealed truth. Television producer Lowell Bergman (Al Pacino) first approaches Jeffrey Wigand (Russell Crowe) as a scientific consultant on a story for the news programme *60 Minutes*. As the former Head of Development at the tobacco company Brown and Williamson, Wigand possesses information proving not only that tobacco is addictive, but also that additives are being used to make it more so. However, Wigand has signed an 'onerous, lifelong confidentiality agreement so stringent he could be in violation if he discussed anything about the corporation' (Brenner 1996). Bergman has to find a way to get around the bind of the agreement, to uncover and broadcast Wigand's knowledge. Although the two men cannot discuss certain facts, they shape their conversations to circumnavigate the agreement, dancing around disclosure.

A consideration of four moments shows how *The Insider* explores the hesitant forging of commitment between two men in publicly charged arenas. On the level of the film's plot, the moments discussed are of great importance. In the first sequence under examination, the film sets up the suspense of whether or not Wigand will respond to Bergman's initial attempts to contact him. In the second, the two men meet for the first time, in a lavish city hotel. In the third moment, and in the protective casing of a car parked on the edge of town, the characters talk around the confidentiality agreement. In the fourth, Bergman's retreat to his beach-house counterpoints Wigand's increasing sense of ensnarement, in the public eye and in returning to the alienating confines of his city hotel room. As the characters' negotiations grow incrementally out of these significant moments, the cityscape shapes their activities.

While not attempting to relate the achievements of *The Insider* to other films by Michael Mann, this analysis is informed by particular remarks made by the critic Jean-Baptiste Thoret, on the collected works of the director. In 'The Aquarium Syndrome', Thoret asserts that:

> Mann is one of those rare filmmakers ... whose films succeed in delivering a vision of modern, urban America: those impersonal places, the freeways, the suburbs, uninterrupted traffic, the America that Baudrillard calls magnificent and sidereal. This is a world of railway yards, neon signs that flicker day and night, a world that seems resigned to the omnipresence of glass and concrete ... Predominant here is the transformation of spaces into 'no-places': hospitals, hotel rooms, roadside cafes, vacant lots, airports, warehouses, empty apartments.
>
> (2002: 1)

Partly in accord with Thoret's claims for the film's interest in the architectural fabric of city spaces, my interpretation does not recognise the collapsing of locations into 'no-places'; rather it claims that each locale is handled differently, as expressing particular grades of closeness and distance, anonymity and intimacy. The first of these locales is the city street. Intrigued by the anonymous delivery of a parcel containing sensitive information on tobacco products, Bergman seeks the assistance of a specialist to 'translate' the documents. He is advised to call Jeff Wigand. Stepping outside a main-street coffee shop, Bergman moves to a street phone, calling Wigand's home.

Immediately, *The Insider* contrasts outlooks of protagonists and places. It shows Bergman's professional ease in the public domain, and Wigand's nervous, reclusive bunkering in his home. The journalist's position on the bustling and bright street is set against the heavy furnishings and shadowy corners of the Wigand household. The exposure of the street setting is amplified by Bergman's use of a particular type of phone. Whereas the cramped confines of a public telephone box afford the user a marginal sense of privacy, the street unit Bergman uses keeps him out in the open. Here, the film hints at how outside interference will impinge on the stuffy composure of the Wigand household. The position of 'the insider' is increasingly connected with the wider world. As the scene progresses, the film also uses location and décor to allude to more established troubles in the Wigand's home. When Wigand's wife answers the phone, a cut takes us inside the lounge. This is a staid space. Rusty browns in the fabric and furnishings blend together to create an insipid environment: this living room is lacking in vitality. The room's want of life connects to the impassive state of the couple's marriage, and Wigand's seemingly blank attitude to the dangerous information he possesses. Bergman's street call stimulates this state, penetrating the muted home space with insistent tones. It is a rude awakening, marking the beginning of Wigand's radicalisation and the two men's relationship.

The tentative union develops as Bergman's professional perseverance raises Wigand's niggled interest, persuading him out of the house, into the open. In their first physical encounter, the two men meet in a city-centre hotel (the Seelbach). The film's decision to set the meeting in a hotel affords the encounter a combination of conflicting associations. The public nature of the setting encourages a sense of the impersonal, existing as an intermediary space. It removes Bergman and Wigand from their everyday locales and offers neutral ground on which to develop their negotiations. The transient nature of the hotel, as a place for short-lived occupancy, matches the transitory relationship of the two characters. The hotel unshackles Wigand from the trappings of the home; in this space, there may be room for manoeuvre.

There are also tensions derived from the danger of discovery. The scene opens with a high-angle shot, as the camera looks down on Bergman sitting in the stately foyer below. Conventionally, this type of shot encourages an idea of surveillance, of someone watching surreptitiously, from a distance, undetected. The film embraces this suggestion, and expands on it. Following Bergman's assured handling of his first verbal contact with Wigand, the shot introduces a note of uncertainty; the feeling that Bergman is being watched threatens the confidentiality of their encounter. It unsettles the consummate fluency of the journalist's professional negotiations, marking an uneasy shift to the anticipated physical meeting. The sense of potential exposure is heightened by the foreboding architecture of a grand hotel. At first, the locale appears ideal for a private meeting. The quiet, sumptuous space of the entrance hall offers a welcome contrast to the bluster and scrabble of the city outside, and a sense of exclusive retreat. Yet, the elaborate marble designs of the enclave are at once imposing and exposing. The hotel's ornate hallway places its residents on display even as it promises austere discretion.

Bergman and Wigand move quickly and quietly towards the more private zone of a hotel suite. The passage to a more intimate space is sealed as the mirrored glass elevator doors slide silently shut, locking the men together. The door's reflective design encourages a sense of close and enclosed security in this snug setting, masking the men's shared escalation to more private discussions, re-bounding the foyer's public outlook. Gliding together, the doors present a final mirrored view of the gleaming marble walls; the shimmering surfaces express an absence of perspective. The city hotel contains its secrets in its surroundings, offering an impression of concealment.

Film and elevator shuttle to explore the levels of intimacy carried by hotel rooms. The suite is especially suited to secret meetings and exclusive celebrations, existing as a pocket of privacy. The film is alert to the particular textures of this grandiloquent space. There is a hermetic quality to the room, caught in the weighty clunk of the door closing shut, the thick and heavy fabric of the curtains, and the wooden solidity of the surrounding furnishings. Bergman uses the sense of airtight security and the reassurance of quality to coax Wigand's confidence. In a series of fluid moves, the journalist opens his travel-bag, drapes his jacket over the hard-back chair, sets down the documents, and signs for coffee. As he controls and centralises his position in this space, Bergman charges the room's design with his authority. Everything is poised for an interview. His gestures exude self-assurance and assertion, marking an encouragement for Wigand to follow suit, to open up. Initially however, the wary scientist presses himself tight to the confines of the room, watching nervously through the window at the streets below, withdrawing into the shadows as room service knocks to enter. The sequence turns on Bergman's attempts to draw Wigand away from the exposure of the window, away from external anxieties, even as he places the scientist in a position of greater vulnerability.

The ensuing interview proves far from satisfactory for the journalist, comprising more intimation than intimate disclosure. Yet it whets his appetite for more, as Wigand nods towards greater truths; when the scientist retreats from the room, the film too hints at possible outcomes, engulfing Wigand in the searing red glow of the corridor, thereby suggesting the incendiary glare of standing in the public spotlight. The final shot of Bergman recalls that of the scientist stood by the window, gazing at the streets below. The rhyme suggests the developing union between the men, now sharing a stance and viewpoint. Here as elsewhere in the film, the glass surface sets up a place of confrontation between enclosure and openness. Following their talk of screened truths and fragile camaraderie, Bergman senses a window of opportunity. At the same time, any further pressure may break the story and the man.

In a third sequence, *The Insider* uses landscape and locale to develop the idea of two men being held together, as both separated from yet vulnerable to the presence of the outer world. Echoing the earlier two moments, the sequence marks a move from personal to public settings. Responding to Wigand's hot-headed attempts to sever ties, Bergman goes to the family home to defend his position. Under duress, Wigand agrees to let the journalist accompany him in the car, to drive out of town.

The geography and geometry of their location express the way the men reach and test the limits of their discussions. Just as the characters' circuitous conversations are bound by the confidentiality agreement, physical barriers and borders frame them together. An ellipse takes us to Wigand's car, now stationed on the fringe of town, and at the water's edge. Both of these borderlines convey the changing circumstances of the two figures, positioned on the verge of disclosure. In the hotel meeting, the characters attempt to find a situation of privacy within the city. As the relationship of the two men progresses, the gravity of their shared situation leads to a withdrawal from the core, towards the more anonymous shadows of an empty warehouse. Yet, crucially, their position remains linked with the metropolis. As the characters sit together in the car, the wider landscape of river and freeway-bridge is seen through the closed windows (see Figure 1.5). The presence of the freeway brings to mind the incessant transit of urban life. On the fringe of the city, even as the two men appear to find a space suited to private dialogue, they are never fully released from mainlines of human traffic. Equally, the rigid straightness of the freeway bridge, and its promise of direct exchange and transfer, forms a taunting visual counterpoint to the roundabout routes of the conversation.

The film develops this suggestion in its coupling of manmade and natural structures. The rigid juts and slats of the bridge hint at the concrete absolutes of the confidentiality agreement. In contrast, the shimmering surface of the water conveys a sense of fluid

Figure 1.5   The Insider (Michael Mann, 1999): Beside the water's edge

indeterminacy in Wigand's position. Ultimately, the glass divide of the car window holds the men from both spaces, just as it exposes. The border of the glass acts as the final barrier of being inside and outside of a situation, separating as much as it connects. As Thoret suggests, 'In Mann's films, glass functions as a plastic extension of the solitude of individuals. The transparency upholds the illusion of communication, but in the end what is evident is the impermeability of spaces' (2002: 9).

The image encapsulates the characters' condition. As the men draw towards a confidence, they are separated from other people, while being exposed to public scrutiny. Through their relationship, both men are cut off from their colleagues, and, in distinct ways, from their families. When they finally go 'on the record' and tape Wigand's interview, their efforts are denied acknowledgement, kept from transmission on TV. The film's handling of urban settings forms the foundations of its expression of two men caught together in states of transition.

In moments of dramatic intensity, the film returns to some of these settings to develop their charge. A fourth and final instance brings together the enclosure of the hotel room and a vast expanse of open water far from Wigand's urban bolt-hole. Associations of closeness and distance heighten as both spaces are bridged by the fragile connection of a mobile phone. When his potentially incendiary television interview is suspended from broadcast, all his efforts apparently wasted, Wigand retreats to his hotel room in feverish paranoia. Caught in the confines of the room, restricted from seeing his family, Wigand turns inward. In a wretched fug, Wigand's frantic mind projects images of his children, melding and morphing across the expanse of the hotel room wall. Calling long-distance from his beach-front apartment, to direct Wigand's attention away from the black depths of delirium and despair – to make him see clearly – Bergman offers a life-line. In 'Delirious Enchantment', Adrian Martin provides a passionate detailing of this fraught scene:

> In ... *The Insider* ... there is a passage so powerful it is almost unbearable. [As] the music is reaching an incredible peak of intensity, the editing gets more frantic as we see the *60 Minutes* reporter Bergman on his mobile phone, trying to reach

[Wigand] – because we, like Bergman – suspect he might be about to kill himself – and then we see the hapless hotel concierge at the end of that conversation on another mobile phone, just outside Wigand's door. The concierge, prompted, tries to get Wigand's attention: no response. 'Tell him to get on the phone', Bergman says. 'I can't do that', says the concierge. Bergman gets louder: 'Tell him to get on the fucking phone!' Finally, the concierge snaps, yelling like a good lad: 'Sir, he says to ... get on the fucking phone!' And then, after all this, Wigand finally moves: he grabs the concierge's mobile, the music stops completely dead on the soundtrack at that instant of contact, and he slams the door.

(2000)

A pivotal connection across great distance creates the moment's dramatic weight: all hangs on the easily broken thread of a mobile phone line. The portable (and so transferable) aspect of the mobile phone allows for the moment in which it is grabbed from the concierge's hands, to be snatched inside Wigand's hotel room, door slammed shut. The mobile momentarily releases Wigand from his circumscribed location and sense of suffocation, creating the semblance of an exclusive channel. From within this pocketed space, the characters speak more freely. The mobile allows the user to roam, moving more freely too. Previously slumped inconsolable in his chair, Wigand now paces the hotel room's corners; Bergman wanders along the water's edge. The film is alert to the way people often allow themselves to drift when speaking on a mobile phone, seemingly without direction, even as their words take a firm route. Straying across the fringe of land and water, bringing Wigand back from the brink, Bergman suddenly takes the plunge. In the blink of a cut, he moves from beach to standing knee-deep in the ocean (see Figure 1.6). In attempting to pull Wigand from a state of dissolution, he loses track of his own direction. The long shot casts the lone figure adrift, black against the formless blue washes of sky and sea: like a little buoy. For once, the magnitude of his circumstances belittles the journalist. He has been drawn in further than he would have liked or intended.

•••

Figure 1.6   The Insider (Michael Mann, 1999): Lost like a little buoy

As the most demonstrative visual element of a film's 'big architecture', the landscape – settings, location, space and place – is often revealed in declamatory measures. In general, films of 'epic' proportion or 'prestige' status use long-shots of sweeping panoramas to heighten the sense of grandeur. As Geoff King argues, the predominant visual form of contemporary Hollywood 'in the age of the blockbuster' presents 'expansive vistas spread out across the width of the big screen' (2000: 1). To use some of King's examples, in films such as *Titanic* (James Cameron, 1997), *Amistad* (Steven Spielberg, 1997), and *Apollo 13* (Ron Howard, 1995), there is a tendency to use the width and breadth of the landscape as a magnificent backdrop, in front of which the characters conduct the business of the film. In contrast, the three films considered in this chapter craft the landscape to express particular and precise facets of their main characters. In some ways, they are smaller films than those cited by King; yet they share the same interest in panoramic shots and 'expansive vistas'. The films are attentive to a series of intertwining relationships: of their understanding and shaping of the wider environment; of the character to the landscape; of the characters to each other within the landscape. Modulations of the tone, fabric, and texture of the landscape convey shifting moods, perspectives, and understandings of the characters. All three films express these shifts and developments in patterning views of landscape and locale. Each return to a particular setting is attuned to the meaning carried in acts of repetition and variation: of landscape composition; in rhymes and adjustments of camera placement and angle; in degrees of lighting, arrangements of décor, and the movements of the characters in and around the settings' spaces.

Sharing a focus on the intricate patterning of place, the films differ in their handling of grand-scale environments. *The Straight Story* sustains views of one man's *situation* in the natural terrain, byways, and towns of Middle America. Through precise arrangements of position (of character) and composition (of landscape), expansive vistas are keyed tightly to the dramatic concerns of the film. In charting an extensive road journey, the film forms patterns in an ever-changing landscape. The film introduces the bigger picture by degrees, while keeping tight to the protagonist and his odd choice of perambulation. Rather than counter Alvin's diminutive position with the grandeur of 'Nature', the move allows the film to gently release views alongside him. The association of one man and the composite surroundings is made closer. In moving towards and away from the mower with equal measures of delicacy, the film personalises the vast tracts of road and field. Progressively, the broad canvas of the landscape is imbued with Alvin's presence.

The Bridges of Madison County concentrates on a smaller number of settings, achieving a sense of expansiveness in the density of its arrangements. The film expresses the significance of change in repeated views of the same setting. Slight modulations to the conveyance of the solid architecture and spaces of the home carry particular resonance. Attention is paid to the characters' crossing and re-crossing of compact spaces within and around the house, on the porch and in the kitchen. Each movement over these spaces marks a passing negotiation, as part of the taut choreography of the characters' relationships. The repetition of moves, back and forth, imbues these domestic spaces with emotion and eroticism. Variations within repetitions express a changing atmosphere within circumscribed settings.

Moving away from the rural settings of the above two films, *The Insider* turns attention to the designs and dimensions of the contemporary urban landscape. It focuses on the way a tentative relationship between two men grows in the anonymous city spaces of Chicago and Louisville. As the characters work to consolidate their relationship, the locations they inhabit accommodate and reflect their efforts. An intricate handling of vast city architecture allows the film to convey particular nuances of trust and restraint. Throughout

The Insider, impersonal spaces and neutral locations – a city street, hotel suite, telephone booth, parking lot – are charged with expressions of intimacy and detachment. In exploring the association between the protagonists and their urban locations, the film blurs the boundaries of the personal and public. These settings form the solid foundations of a precarious relationship.

2
Gesture

The Insider

Dancing around disclosure

Throughout *The Insider*, the legal weight of the confidentiality agreement prevents Bergman and Wigand from directly discussing hugely consequential information. Locked in intense discussion, the men are held apart by the document. As the confidentiality agreement hems and defines the characters' negotiations, their gestures express a negotiation of obstacles (legal, linguistic, physical, and emotional). As they are unable to ask certain questions or provide certain answers, the two men *gesture towards* the truth. The characters clarify or obscure their standpoint and greater implications in their poise, stance, and posture, in each narrowing of the eyes or fidget of hands. As well as conveying a shifting relationship to surrounding barriers, the two men's gestures express the gradual development of their friendship. Through gesture, the film conveys particular levels of engagement coming within – as a consequence of the confidentiality agreement – an enforced state of inaction.

Restriction and control

In the separate opening views of Bergman and Wigand, *The Insider* introduces distinct forms of composure in imposing situations. It first concentrates on the journalist, as he travels under guard to interview the leader of the Hezbollah, Sheikh Fadlallah. Bergman's initial situation – blindfolded, sat in the back of a car, en route to an undisclosed location – places him in a position of restriction, submission, and dependence: a physical foil to his later verbal station with Wigand. On entering the gloomy confines of the rendezvous, Bergman is guided to his chair, to face his awaiting interviewee. The film's introduction of Bergman contrasts with its subsequent presentation of a character in control, a high-profile agent of television, a consummate creator of scenarios. The clout of this 'mover and shaker' initially appears heavily restricted. Yet, in a set of limited hand gestures, the character conveys his ability to manage situations from a position of constraint. His handling of the scenario forms a prelude to his later management of forcefully bound negotiations.

To secure a recorded interview, the TV journalist directs his body in concentrated gestures of persuasion. Any visual entreaty that would be encouraged by facial expression is denied by the hood over his head. The force of his appeal is carried in clipped phrases and three slight moves of his hand. As Bergman speaks of the 'integrity and objectivity' of *60 Minutes*, his left hand moves to rest on his leg. Ever so slightly, the journalist pushes his weight forwards, without overly pressing a point. As he moves, his right hand taps down in the air, lightly accentuating the words 'highly rated, most respected'. Awaiting an answer, Bergman then rests his hands together in his lap. The impression of calm composure is only troubled by a passing curl and press of fingers to thumb: a pinch of anxiety. This fleeting gesture of 'tightening up' gathers and contains the tensions in the room.

With the interview quietly and abruptly agreed, the sense of containment is met by two gestures of release and exposure. Perceiving the Sheikh's silent exit, Bergman removes his blindfold. The effect of 'seeing clearly' is complemented by the character's move to cast open the gloomy room's shrouding curtains, suddenly exposing a majestic cityscape below (see Figure 2.1). Bergman's gestures express the act of a figure decisively revealing the world to himself (rather than having it revealed to him). A restrained position in front of the Hezbollah gives way to a more assertive and pronounced form of composure. The bright city vista, once concealed, now revealed from behind the curtain, appears as a carefully timed climactic tableau to Bergman's little play of persuasion. As the curtains open, sunlight and street sounds spill into the room like validating applause for the television producer's efforts. As Bergman moves onto the balcony, he sweeps his hair from his eyes, and presses a mobile phone to his ear, connecting with and reasserting his place in the wider world.

Figure 2.1   The Insider (Michael Mann, 1999): The city revealed from behind the curtain

As the first sequence ends with an assertion of Bergman's connection with the world, the opening views of Wigand show him held from his wider surrounds, contained and sealed off. The recently dismissed scientist is framed in the sound-proof window of his office at Brown and Williamson, divided from his now ex-colleagues. Returning home, Wigand first performs a move of fluent control. Passing swiftly through the lounge, and with a cursory greeting to his daughter, he arcs around the drinks bar, tipping just the right amount of ice into a glass, pouring a neat whiskey. The precision and fluidity of the move suggests that pouring a drink after work is a regular occurrence, performed at the close of each day. As this particular day is far from routine, the easy move also acts as a gesture of solace, of preparation for coming worries. The effortless route to the bar serves to smooth away the ruffles of anxiety. While all else is uncertain, at least the drink is fixed.

The controlled composure of a neat measure is held in tension with a developing strain, of indirect glances and gestures. As the whiskey allows Wigand a welcome point of focus, he casts only brief looks at his daughter before returning to his glass. His words – 'A little too early for cartoons, isn't it?' – are spoken with a quickly disappearing half-smile. As Wigand conceals his anger at his professional situation, he tucks the rage into a mild remonstration. (It is also a prim deflection of any unspoken criticism; it seems it is not 'a little too early' for whiskey.) In gestures patterned throughout the film,

Wigand searches for composure, stroking down his tie and pushing his glasses up on his nose. The bulk of his body rests uneasily with these pernickety moves. Restrained from any demonstrative action by the powers of the tobacco corporation, and in the face of his family, Wigand is reduced to redundant little measures of comfort, fussiness, and correction.

The first exchange between the two men is performed in gestures each unseen by the other. As entreaties for attention by telephone are ignored, Bergman tries to raise Wigand by fax. The journalist's manner in composing the first fax expresses an edgy determination. His writing is fast and without hesitation; the imperative manner of his action is underlined by his brusquely tossing the pen aside, hurrying to place the page in the machine. As a response finally arrives, slowly sliding out, Bergman reaches out his fingers to tug at the paper in anticipation. Pens, fingers, and paper: there is an intimate, tactile connection between the two players; yet, at this stage, it remains indirect, mediated by technology and removed from the immediacy of a spoken conversation. The paper acts as a silent invitation for more direct engagement: it seems Wigand is now in a position to speak. Grabbing the phone to set up the hotel rendezvous, a further gesture by Bergman crystallises the complexity of his relationship to the other man, at just this point. Placing his glasses down on the desk, Bergman's hand suddenly returns to them, darting towards, yet not quite touching, the fragile lenses. It is a move of reassurance, at once affirming that the glasses will not fall, while betraying a necessary preparation, just in case they do. It is a startled act quickly redressed into a display of control. Turning alarm to a useful state of alertness, Bergman applies an exacting measure of readiness to a matter of delicacy.

As the film finally brings the men together in the hotel suite, contrasting measures of agility and uncertainty set the relationship in motion. Bergman conjures with the trappings to hand. Objects are handled with swagger and confidence. A curt question from Wigand ('Why here?') is met by a smooth flourish of papers; the door is opened the instant room service knocks to enter, like the final reveal of a much-rehearsed trick; a pen appears as if by magic to sign the tab. In sleight of hand, Bergman attempts to draw out testier truths through diversion. In contrast with the range and display of the producer's moves, Wigand first draws tight to the confines of the room. His sturdy build is stilled, pressed tight against the shadowy, reassuringly solid structure of the wall. Gradually, Bergman's conceit of confidence inspires cautious assurance, and Wigand is drawn into the centre of the room. Sitting with Bergman, the two discuss the scientific documents, and share coffee.

The commonplace ritual act of sharing coffee creates an intermediary, normalising focal point, allowing the men to concentrate on, and negotiate through, an everyday activity. It offers the characters a defensive position from behind which to consider the position of the other. As the men exchange comments, they take sips of the coffee, each sip punctuating (and so underscoring) the weight of their remarks. Equally, within the exchange, Bergman uses his sipping at the cup to conceal an upward turn of the head, focusing his inquisitive gaze on Wigand. At the same time, the lack of a rattling saucer stands as testimony to his calm nature, while Wigand abandons his cup, sitting upright with hands clasped together, in a defensive posture.

Throughout the sequence, the shaping and positioning of Wigand's body expresses a restlessly unsure stance. While prone to telltale twitches of hands and face (a tic as room service enters, a twinge as Bergman tries small-talk), the solidity of his physique creates an incongruent presence of strength and force. Aspects come together in his sitting posture, betraying an anxious temperament. He perches uncomfortably on his chair, his bulky frame caught in awkward angles. His poise conveys a lack of commitment to, and shades of distractedness from, each situation. In slight shifts and adjustments, Wigand's body expresses the character's ongoing struggle to settle on a position that sits well with his conscience.

Wigand's attempts at control and composure inspire scrutiny; as Adam Phillips remarks, 'Composure, like a dare, sustains and challenges the idea of accurate recognition' (2000: 45). As Wigand studies the documents, Bergman is invited, dared, to study him with equal intensity. A supposedly final, finalising gesture further 'sustains and challenges the idea of accurate recognition'. Closing the book of documents, Wigand announces 'That's as far as I go.' He drops the book onto the table, patting and smoothing his hand on his leg. The gesture is complex. At once, it appears as a touch of decisiveness and finality, a 'brushing off' of business. At the same time, the gesture echoes Wigand's stroke of his tie, as a little defence against recrimination. Equally, it hints at a need to keep things in place. Declaring he will go no further suggests there is further to go. Open to interpretation, Wigand's hand gesture combines with the inference of the remark. An apparent conclusion encourages further attention and keeps matters in play.

The Bridges of Madison County

Stiffness to sensuality

As the dramatic pitch of *The Insider* is refined by gesture, the low-key affair of *The Bridges of Madison County* is intensified with an intricate mesh of physical moves. The film emphasises the rich sensuality of the affair as the scenes taking place in the 'present' work in counterpoint to those of Francesca and Robert in 1965. There is a flatness and crudeness to the handling of the present-day scenarios, playing against and underscoring a textural depth of the sequences set in the past. Consider the way the film handles the (grown) children's discovery of Francesca's secret mementos. The camera peers down on the lid of a timber chest that fills the frame, before creaking open to reveal the box's neatly packed contents. Choices of angle and framing emphasise the lid's flat woodenness. In turn, the film leads into the moment of discovery with a sense of inflexibility, furthered in aspects of performance. A low-angle shot reveals Carolyn hunkering down, warily unpacking items from the chest. Michael is adjacent, upright, arms folded, eyes fixed front. As more details of Francesca's affair are revealed, the rigidity of the son's position increases. The film emboldens the sense of austerity, as the taut frame of Michael's body stands firm against a series of corresponding vertical lines: the lid of the chest, the bed-frame, and the struts of the bedroom window (see Figure 2.2). Critics have previously bemoaned the 'wooden' nature of the children's performances.[1] Here though, the film successfully uses the inflexibility of Slezak, matching his brittle presence with hard lines and frames to create a declamatory expression of flatness and stiffness.

While the scene could easily give itself over to wide-eyed wonderment of Francesca's colourful past, it boldly sustains a sense of neutrality. Again, this is felt in the presence of the children, of these two performers. Just as the film considers the weight of Eastwood and Streep's personas, it acknowledges and makes use of Slezak and

Figure 2.2 The Bridges of Madison County (Clint Eastwood, 1995): A stiff joint

Corley's anonymity. They appear as ciphers, hollow signifiers of the 'present' as an empty time (in comparison with the emotional richness of their mother's past experiences). The sense is carried in the matching neutral shades of the children's khaki clothing, blending into the bedroom's muted greys and greens. There is paleness to the siblings' presence in this room, in their pallid complexions and strained reactions to lively discoveries. The sounds of the scene complement the colours; the pair's voices are dulled in the air. The occasional lone twitter of a bird from the fields points up the stillness of the setting. The only other tone of life comes as Carolyn unpacks Francesca's copy of *National Geographic*. The famous yellow stripes of the magazine's cover add a brief glow, announcing the first glimpse of Robert Kincaid pictured inside the edition. Retaining the stark lifelessness of the instant, the film quietly introduces a tinge of a brighter past. As the scene moves to a moment from 1965 and the introduction of Francesca, the flicker and density of colour carries into a concentration of gesture.

Containment and release (Francesca)

In the very first view of Francesca, as she prepares the family's dinner, sliding fried food from stove to plate, the film hints at the pressures of her place in the world. The air is thick with the hiss and spit of the frying pan, and the incessant chirrup of crickets outside. Resting the pan solidly on the hob, Francesca makes a move away from the stove and towards the radio. Her physical response to the music marks a momentary, measured release of pressure. The aria appears to beckon her, pulling her briefly away from preparations. Turning up the volume, Francesca lightly closes her eyes and tips her head in a gentle dip. With a gesture to be seen again in the film, she smoothly strokes at the air with her hand, as if putting the final touch to an unseen signature. She *conducts* the music, in flowing gestures guiding and being guided by soothing tones. There is a comfortably paired lightness in the movement of aria and character; both clash with the prior heavy clunk of cooking pans. Having drawn breath with the music, Francesca returns to the steam of the stove.

The delicacy of Francesca's response to the aria contrasts with her edgy reaction to three more sounds; jolts of gesture and noise announce the family's clattering arrival. While the family coming together unsettles the restless housewife, each noise and response is carefully measured. First, the son's arrival is gruffly declared in the porch door's bang against the jamb. Already tense, Francesca's shoulders jerk at the sound. As agitated by the slam's shock as the act's recurrence, she rebukes her son with the words 'Michael, what've I told you about that door?' At the same time, her gestures convey a greater containment of feeling. Before scolding her son, Francesca lifts her eyes to the wall and leans down to scoop up a bowl of food, turning to set the serving squarely on the table. In the dip of her body, Francesca pushes down a bellyful of frustration. As her husband enters, the door bangs again. Francesca jolts once more, hands darting towards her face. Checking herself, she smoothes away the urge to react; her palm pats at the air as if pressing things down, setting things in place. The daughter comes in last, striding into the room and towards the radio, turning the dial to find a different tune. Already punctuated by the door's loud bangs, the graceful aria now crackles away to Pop. Initially opening her mouth to react, Francesca instead busies herself with setting down the cutlery. The quick fizz of white noise between radio stations channels her agitation.

While the family silently sets to work on the dinner, with the crockery's heavy chunk and clink replacing any signs of meal-time chatter, Francesca springs to her feet to collect a forgotten jug. Her body is set, here and at points through the film, against solid bulky objects: the tall white refrigerator, a chest of drawers, the covered bridges of Madison County. Most immediately, the film contrasts the restlessness of the character with the fixity of the objects or markers of her world. Yet, while expressive of the weight of Francesca's surroundings, the objects are placed in a more complex relationship with the character through gesture. Consider the way Francesca retrieves the jug from the refrigerator and closes the heavy metal door with her foot, clipping it with just the right amount of pressure in a spirited turn of the heel. Later, as Francesca eases out the bedroom dresser's stuck drawer, she informs her husband that 'you can't get mad at it'. Rather than fighting against the fixed and weighty trappings of her world, Francesca finds a way to work with them. In physical meeting points with surface and mass, she uses the objects' load to push down her feelings while allowing herself little measured releases of tension, spent in each swing of the fridge door and slide of the drawer.

These are gestures of necessity but also more. Setting the jug on the table, Francesca nimbly raises her hand to flick a fly away from her face. It is sensible to imagine that in the humid setting of the Midwest such a gesture is oft repeated, instinctive. Here, an enigmatic charm touches the perfunctory action. The path taken by Francesca's hands through the air echoes her tracing the sign of the cross moments before. Brushing away a constantly droning disturbance takes grace.

The character's hands are employed throughout the sequence in fidgety action: fetching and carrying food, dabbing at the air, swatting away the fly. With the final, forgotten item now placed on the dinner table, Francesca anxiously attempts to settle down to the meal. Her hands flutter hesitantly about her face as she tilts and turns her head. They search for a place to rest, just as the character wavers in the various settings of the film, quietly uncertain of an appropriate position. In the scene's closing moments, Francesca bridges her hands under her chin, ready to dip her head. Yet rather than sink down, she seeks refuge in the pop song on the radio. With a tiny smile, Francesca lifts and turns her head to the side, as her fingers reach up to tease at the bun of her hair. As well as offering comfort, the music and gesture mark a momentary withdrawal. Releasing her attention from the family for a second, Francesca loosens her hair, but only slightly.

In the final moments of the sequence, Francesca's anxieties remain checked, held in a measured gesture. Moving to follow her husband out of the bedroom, she pauses for a beat, tapping once on the top of the dresser with the tips of her fingers. As Francesca pats the dresser, it answers with a thick tone. The sound offers comfort in its solidity, while also expressing the density and permanence of the trappings that surround the character. The action is nimbly performed. It marks the end of Francesca's preparations for her family's visit to the State Fair, as a 'job well done'. The gesture is also indicative of a need to touch base. With a gentle tap to the solid wooden object, Francesca is keeping things in check, reassuring herself that everything is held firmly and fixedly in place. Again, she works *with* the heavy trappings of her world to get through the day. She contains the burden of her chores in a compact gesture, lightly released against the weight of the dresser.

Transience and fixity (Robert)

In his profession as a travelling photographer, Robert journeys from place to place without settling down. The film presents a delicate quality to Robert's presence and moves, as he drifts into and out of Madison County. His *appearance* is amorphous, unfixed.[2] The surrounding sense of Robert's lack of grounding expresses and informs the evanescence of the four-day affair. As he washes under an outdoor shower (spied on by Francesca from her bedroom window), the water brings a fluid sheen to his leathery body. As the couple converse in the kitchen later that evening, smoke from Francesca's cigarette drifts across her view of the photographer. The smoke's glide and curlicue are as gently bewitching as the magical fact of Robert's apparition, and as easily broken. If the mood were to alter by the slightest touch, the stranger might vanish 'in a puff of smoke'. Under Roseman Bridge's arch, Robert suddenly appears and disappears from view, leaving only his camera's tripod behind. (We will return to this moment and sequence in Chapter 6.)

Yet, in the form and economy of his gestures, Robert searches for ways to secure a hold, however temporary, on a passing situation. To counteract his wider lack of grounding, in passing moves, the character attempts to gain a grip on the world around him. He constantly searches for closeness with his environment and things to hand. Each move is a small step in an unfamiliar environment, performed as a little stay. The majority of his gestures are task-driven: functionally conceived, measured, and performed. Consider his initial moves outside the truck, on reaching Roseman Bridge with Francesca. Leaning into the hold of the truck, Robert flips open his work-bag and lifts out a camera and tripod. The equipment is found and readied without fuss: without a rummaging through or upsetting of the container, or a clumsy grappling with the tripod's long heavy legs. A workaday move is achieved without appearing laboured. Robert exercises a sure touch. As the tripod is lifted out of the hold, the photographer snaps the metal struts together in a neat 'clack'. Gesture and sound form a punctuation mark, denoting the end of the task and the beginning of a wider charge, of shooting the bridge. It also marks a move away from Francesca, as Robert's attention channels towards his work. Moving the camera and tripod, Robert clicks into gear. In turn, Francesca is cast adrift, without useful purpose, wandering across and through the bridge. A momentary task, decisively performed, directs the manner of the characters' broader negotiations.

The gesture echoes and deepens the effect of an earlier instance, as the couple sat together in the truck on the way to the bridge. In this prior moment, as the conversation pauses and in search of his cigarettes, Robert reaches his arm across the housewife's lap, stretching towards the glove-box. Through and within the task of retrieving the cigarettes, Robert's arm presses lightly against Francesca's leg ('Excuse me'). Francesca responds by lifting her hands in a gesture of politely proclaimed withdrawal. Robert's reach meets the film's decision to shift to close-up. Both moves mark momentary assertions; both press gently towards familiarity. A glint of Robert's silver wrist bracelet adds a grade more substance to the move; in this and other instances, its burnished appearance delicately encourages attention. Towards the end of the film and after Robert's death, the return of the bracelet to Francesca gathers together memories of the affair. It is a lasting marker of his ephemeral company and passing gestures. In other instances, the lighting of a cigarette nimbly points up particular moments shared by the couple. As their first day together draws to a close, Robert's flick and snap of his thumb to the lifting flame punctuates the drowsy quiet of the evening. At points, the repeated gesture marks a shift between 'past' and 'present', as the film's story snaps back and forth. As with the sight of the bracelet, the clipped sound and flicker of the lighter's flame mark a passing of time and memorialise moments.

A further tension arises, of the surrounding gliding quality of Robert's presence, and the solidity sensed in moments of immobility. As the significance of Robert's spare gestures accrues across the film, a charge carries around the character's occasional stillness. To return to the first moves on Roseman Bridge, as Robert readies his camera and tripod he steps purposefully down the slope of a hill, finding a good position from which to capture the view. The movement is capped by a sense of fixity, of setting down the tripod and pivoting the camera from a set position. Whereas in some circumstances inactivity suggests apathy (as forms of 'doing nothing' or 'going nowhere'), in this instance Robert's stillness forms a charged centre of gravity, drawing the attention of Francesca's glimpses and glances (as detailed in Chapter 6). The film is attentive to the influence of Eastwood's persona. As Dennis Bingham notes, Eastwood's heroes are ordinarily 'so immobile that motionlessness becomes equated with strength' (1994: 223). The film gathers all of these aspects in the final view of Robert, standing silent in the storm. As the lovers glimpse each other for the last time across a rain-slicked street, the photographer presents a final snapshot of himself before disappearing beyond Winterset's limits. This climactic sequence is shaped into a series of small moves, delicate and taut. Its bearing turns on the sparseness and simplicity of Robert's closing gestures. As Francesca returns from the convenience store, tipping with the heavy grocery bag into the truck, she gradually becomes aware of Robert's presence across the way. Held first in the opacity of the truck's wet window, the foggy vision becomes a little clearer as she tilts her head, peering at Robert through the swirling rain. The water's liquid mist accentuates the spectral aspect of this lone figure. He is cast in a thinned, translucent image, flimsy in the film of the rain.

On the edge of town, the passing encounter is marked by boundaries of restricted gestures. The 'stranger' stands stiff by his truck. As his rigid presence is finally acknowledged, Robert moves forwards, towards Francesca, in four short steps. The succinct measure of moves expresses his precise standing towards the moment; he is determined, yet not pressing. Falling still again, Robert appears steadfast. Now unmoving, for Francesca the gesture stirs emotion and inspires new hesitations. She manages a slight smile; he smiles too but turns to go. Almost imperceptibly, she shakes her head. Robert does not falter in his moves, yet the moment is filled with a wider sense of doubt; the promise of certainty dissolves in the rain. The wavering of Francesca's half-smile and quaver carry a greater vacillation, between staying firm and moving on.

Two final gestures seal the moment and carry the weight of the film. As Francesca's husband returns to the truck, they wait at the traffic lights, drawing close behind Robert's own vehicle. Through the frame of the back window, Robert slowly winds a fine silver chain around the rear-view mirror. Focusing in, Francesca recognises the chain as her necklace, given to Robert on their final day together. The chain holds a cross, now dangling from the mirror, swinging to count down the changing of the traffic light, from red, to green. Again, a keepsake carries the resonance of the affair. Even now, the conclusion of the relationship remains suspended with the silver cross. In Robert's gesture of threading the chain around the mirror, the film gently plays not only with the idea of a climactic moment being wound up, but also the characters' emotional constriction. The suggestion is matched in Francesca's responding move; gradually her hand curls right around the car door's release mechanism. The coiled tension of the mechanism's spring is tested to breaking point; ultimately, heartbreakingly, Francesca yields, and the trucks separate. The film marks the stark fact and pain of the separation in its wider views. As Robert moves beyond the limits of the town, the gentle inference of his gestures is replaced with the harsh assertion of mechanical pointers: the traffic light switches colour; the indicator blinks and flares, solidly, intently signalling Robert's direction away from Francesca.

The Age of Innocence

Catching at moments

Set in the 1870s, *The Age of Innocence* charts the affairs of New York aristocracy. It tells the story of Newland Archer (Daniel Day Lewis), who is to be married to May Welland (Winona Ryder), of the powerful Mingott clan. On the eve of the engagement being announced, the Wellands reintroduce a disgraced member of their family to Society: Countess Ellen Olenska (Michelle Pfeiffer). Smitten by the new arrival, Newland is increasingly torn between his love for the Countess and the commitments of his preordained life with May.

Although the intense relationship between Newland Archer and Ellen Olenska undulates through every frame of *The Age of Innocence*, it is not presented as a continuous thread of action, coursing from scene to consecutive scene. Rather, the film traces the daily histories of the grand families of New York. The meetings between Newland and Ellen are momentary happenings within a greater set of social circumstances, in particular, other events involving Newland.

The childhood acquaintances are first reintroduced at the opera, the chosen venue for Ellen's grand return into the upper echelons of New York Society. Whereas this first encounter is bound up in a formal welcome, with Newland making his way up to the opera box to pay his respects, the second meeting occurs on the cusp of a departure. It takes the form of a passing exchange, as Newland and May bid farewell to Mrs Mingott (Miriam Margoyles), just as Ellen enters with Julius Beaufort (Stuart Wilson) – as addressed in Chapter 3. Following the informal passing-through at Mrs Mingott's house, the Duke of St Austrey Dinner returns the couple to the oppressive environs of a grand occasion. After the meal, Ellen risks gossip by crossing the room to talk privately with Newland. The pair then manage to meet several times privately at Ellen's apartment. A later attempt at privacy in imposing social circumstances places them together again in the setting of the opera, at the performance of 'The Shaughraun'.[3] This brief meeting of two guests forms another encounter happening on the periphery of a Society event. After Newland's marriage to May, his meetings with Ellen become less frequent and more abstracted. The lovers catch at moments of shared time, always on the move: at the Blenker House, in a carriage, in the art museum, at Ellen's farewell dinner.

Their encounters punctuate the narrative, rather than dictate it. Yet, the significance of each fragmentary meeting is felt. *The Age of Innocence* repeatedly achieves a sense of momentousness in a meeting's brevity. Initially, the shortness of encounters suggests not only how significant relationships may grow from and within passing experiences, but also how infrequency can intensify feelings. By necessity, the later meetings must remain brief, and, in public, they must appear innocuous, for fear of the couple being discovered. The possibility of exposure impresses itself on each instant, just as the desire to prolong the moment becomes ever more pronounced.

Gesture is crucial to both the film's and characters' handling of curtailed rendezvous. Under scrutiny, two particular meetings open up as distinct fragments (contained within different social occasions) and as bound by a fine line of continuity, woven in gestural patterns. As both instances take place in a public arena, Newland and Ellen shape each socially asserted and assertive move to conceal an offering of intimacy.

A momentary suspension

In our first views of Countess Olenska, Michelle Pfeiffer performs two gestures that are at once declamatory and intimate.[4] Prior to this moment, we have only seen Ellen in two fleeting long shots, through the inquisitive lens of Larry Lefferts's (Richard E. Grant) lorgnettes. Lefferts devotes himself to training his eye on the conduct of New York Society. With a start, he catches a glimpse of Ellen as she enters the opera box, dipping down into her seat. Alerted to Ellen's presence by Lefferts's biting commentary, Newland ascends the stairs to the Wellands's private enclave, greeting his fiancé, her mother, and the returned Countess. Rather than convey the moment of reacquaintance as a gentle prelude to a kindling relationship, the film explores the particular way in which Newland is held by Ellen's charm. A moment of confusion develops to reveal measures of enchantment. The opening view of Ellen hints at her particular appeals. The camera gradually carries towards the Countess, and a blurred background of the opera audience washes into view. The movement sets her blue dress against a sea of black suits punctuated with white breastplates. At once, the view contrasts Ellen's singular presence with that of the crowd's monochrome uniformity.

Time stretches in two extensions of Ellen's arm, first to Newland in greeting, then over the throngs below. When the Countess raises her hand to be kissed, she is unprepared for an awkward reaction, and causes a moment of embarrassment. Through a clipped series of cuts, her hand hangs in the air, waiting to be embraced. As Newland finally decides to shake hands instead, the film moves out to long shot, showing Ellen's arm remaining aloft, uncertain (see Figure 2.3). The movement through different views elongates the moment, emphasising its awkwardness. Ellen is a little shaken; regaining composure, her second gesture slows the moment more emphatically and draws Newland closer. Expressing delight at her return to New York's

Figure 2.3   *The Age of Innocence* (Martin Scorsese, 1993): Ellen embarrassed

high social echelons, she gracefully passes her fan over the spectators below. It appears at once as a token of fondness for her environment, and of dominion. With a single wave of the fan, Ellen casts a spell over the galleries. Moving out to long shot, the film gently releases the spell, while opening up a view that conveys the gesture's delicate hold over Ellen's new confidant. A single trace of blue light cuts through the background of suited spectators towards the stage. The cobalt beam is the bright ray of a stage spotlight; it also appears as a vestige of Ellen's enchantment: a trace of the fan's glide, and an effusion of her iridescent blue outfit. The charm of the moment hangs in the air; this time, for Newland, the effects of a declamatory gesture linger pleasurably on.

After a beat, the camera withdraws, swooping down into the orchestra pit on a drum roll. The film refocuses its attention on the stage where Faust's pursuit of the innocent Marguerite reaches its climax. It elects not to show the separation of Newland and Ellen at the opera's close, moving from the audience's applause to the narrator's (Joanne Woodward) first comments on society as Mrs Julius Beaufort's rising from her seat indicates that 'half an hour later, the annual Beaufort Ball would begin'. An emphasis is placed on removal: images dissolve from opera house to ballroom. Against the tide of these orchestrations, the scenario of the lovers' first meeting is caught in time, free from the discomposure of the couple taking their leave and bidding farewell. Not for the last time, a passing hold on intimacy is overtaken by wider schemes of silent signals.

Directions of attention

The tension of a passing encounter at once seemingly inconsequential, publicly performed, and privately significant lies at the heart of the couple's relationship. It reaches its apogee in the moment of Ellen's move towards Newland at the Duke of St Austrey Dinner. The meeting is significant for more than one reason, but particularly in the context of gesture because Ellen replays the handshake to the amusement of both. After Ellen is snubbed by society at a planned Mingott dinner, the Van der Luydens – the leaders of that society – make an unmistakeable gesture in response. Ellen is invited to their dinner as another opportunity to reassert her position within New York aristocracy. Consequently, she becomes the undeclared centre of attention. A sense of circumspect, collective observation heightens the effect of her direct move across the room (see Figure 2.4). As the film's narrator observes, 'It was not the custom in New York Society for a woman to leave one man and cross the room for another.' Rather, as Wharton's novel continues, the woman should 'wait, immovable as an idol, while the men who wished to converse with her succeeded each other at her side' (1948: 60). Yet, as Joy L. Davis remarks, 'Ellen ... not comprehending the concept of a passive "angel", audaciously solicits an interview with Archer' (1993: 471–2).

Ellen's move advances her relationship with Newland, intensifying the possibilities of shared time. Echoing the effect of the opera-box meeting, the act forms a sudden fascination, awkwardly conceived.

Figure 2.4   The Age of Innocence (Martin Scorsese, 1993): Ellen makes her move

Here, a brief passage of slowed movement contains the moment's draw. The decision to use the declarative, protracting technique of slow motion, at this point, is well judged. It registers the momentous impact that Ellen's daring gesture has on the amassed elite, like a collectively drawn breath. The film achieves this sensation without having to recourse to close-up shots of shocked faces or muttering cliques. The effect on the group is felt in the suggestive use of a stylistic device trained on the individual. Ellen rises from her seat into the flow of slow motion, as if stepping serenely into a gale. The effect is one of graceful calm, folding within it the overwhelming significance of her gesture. As the Countess draws near to Newland, the film alters the speed to convey a quickening of emotion. The camera arcs around, connecting the characters; the fluid move hastens the tempo without breaking continuity. It is a final rush, conveying at once the guests' quietly scandalised comprehension, and a quickening of the couple's pulses on the cusp of a greeting.

Having brought us to the point of this crucial public meeting with meticulous measure, the film composes the brief exchange with acuity. Responding to the change in pace, the camera holds still on the couple as they sit together. Through its arrangements, the moment appears suspended in private time. In focusing closely on just these two characters, the camera's position tucks them away from the greater activity of the dinner. As Leslie Stern suggests, 'The Countess Ellen Olenska moves across the room in a trajectory that erases the vastness of space and simultaneously opens up an aporia' (1995: 225). Shaping the moment with senses of suspension and enclosure, it is as if the film creates a bubble, affording the characters short-lived sanctuary. The sound tapers to enhance the suggestion, filtering the ripples of the inquisitive collective.

At the same time, the wider community's presence remains implicitly apparent. Although the camera fixes the couple tight into their private corner, the angle shows the characters looking out intermittently onto the room. Again, the film expresses the full impact of the couple's rendezvous without adopting a forceful stance. All the surreptitious interest of the party-goers is distilled in the camera's *particular* position: shooting a sideways look at the couple. As at the opera, the meeting is held in a tension of public scrutiny and private shelter. For the characters, the delicate balance proves impossible to sustain. The bubble has to burst.

The moment's exclusivity breaks just as the conversation reaches a quiet climax:

Newland: You know, you're amongst friends here.
Ellen: Yes, I know, that's why I came home.

As the camera absorbs Ellen's purposeful response, fixing on her smile, a soft trip of footsteps bleeds into the soundtrack. May's entrance into the room is introduced as whisperingly intrusive. The sound of her nimble tread and the rustle of her gown scuffle into the muted chamber, across the rhythm of a piano interlude. The patter is heard before May is seen; the camera's gaze lingers on Ellen. In an instant, the film delicately binds the two women, just as it punctures the sealed sanctuary. The fact of May's arrival in the room, and her coterie's bustling fuss-making over her appearance, indirectly interrupt the couple's conversation; its completion is sealed as Mr Van der Luyden (Michael Gough) cuts in, presenting the Countess to another guest. Ellen hurriedly arranges a further rendezvous with Newland, proposing a firm date ('tomorrow afternoon'). Despite his prior ignorance of any such plan, he quickly accedes, in step with Ellen's game. Standing to bid the Countess farewell, Newland rises to the occasion.

Finally, the film allows all the sensed interest of the group in this private conversation to crystallise in a single wry look. Turning from Ellen draws Newland back into the room's throng. As if on cue, Larry Lefferts, the epicentre of tittle-tattle, passes Newland with a smile and shining eyes. The move also encapsulates the furtive quality of the group's interest and the film's evocation of such silent scrutiny; Lefferts slithers past Newland at the back of the frame, apparently deep in discussion with his companion and barely in focus: it is a glancing act. A more forceful intervention occurs as Mrs Van der Luyden (Alexis Smith) suddenly arches in from the right, across elaborately bunched curtains. The suggestion of her 'waiting in the wings' for Newland's removal from Ellen comes through in her words; she has orchestrated her husband's interruption, turning Newland's attention back to his betrothed:

It was good of you to devote yourself to Madame Olenska so unselfishly, dear Newland. I told Henry he really must rescue you. I think I've never seen May looking lovelier.

Her arrangements are as exquisitely overbearing as the room's heavy décor; a moment of inappropriate privacy is halted in a meticulously executed gesture and icily kind words.

Motions of fixity

Before Newland's marriage to May, the clandestine couple are bound on a path of forward planning, wistfully disregarding the immediate present in hope of the future. After the wedding, Newland tries to immerse himself in each stolen moment with Ellen. The attempt comes too late. Instead of sharing a current of continuity, the brief meetings are linked by a shared aspect of futility, of Newland's efforts to gather the disparate moments as they ebb away. One instant conveys the paradox of the lovers' situation most distinctly. Again, the film's attention to gesture carries the complexity of the couple's relationship.

Newland's desire to conserve moments with Ellen is explicitly addressed in his decision to 'save' an afternoon in Boston ('Oh I think for a change I'll just save it, instead of spending it'). The idea of a saved afternoon combines the desire to savour the passing moment with a wish to preserve it. Taking his leave from May and his family, Newland searches for Ellen in Boston, to capture some time with her. The film infuses the scene of their meeting with Newland's want for fixedness. As the couple sit side by side on the park bench, he bargains with her ('Just give me the day'). Acceding, Ellen is encouraged to write a note to cancel her appointment with Monsieur Rivière (Jonathan Pryce). As Newland presents her with his 'new stylographic' pen to write the note, a slight gesture encapsulates the occasion's desperate intensity. As the camera looms over the bench, Newland stabs the pen in the air, loosening the ink. After recoiling from the action, Ellen scratches Rivière's name on the card. There is a sense of alarm contained in the moment's animation.

The act is charged with Newland's quietly frenzied purpose. It is performed as an entreaty, of Ellen signing a contract to spend (or 'save') the afternoon with him alone. As well as providing a sense of assuredness, the deed allows Newland to believe he is somehow able to preserve or own this brief passage of time. As the afternoon progresses, the idea of a fixed bond with the hour is shown to be hopelessly misconceived. As the couple sit on the veranda, time inevitably slips away. As the narrator states, in the dying moments of the day, 'all human presence and vitality is faded out'. In two dissolves, the characters slowly disappear from the setting.

•••

As the films focus on the characters' relationships in and with their settings, attention is also given to the performance of gesture in a wider scenario. Gesture at once appears a diminutive element of a film's arrangements, yet it can carry great significance. It is also an element of film style normally associated with aspects of intimacy, inextricably connected with the performer's body and, in turn, *in touch* with humanly responsive actions and reactions. The films discussed above combine all of these associations; they explore the integration, counterpoint, emphasis, and concealment of gesture through moments, patterns, and other points of style. In certain instances, a dominant assertion of weight and significance – of a vast or elaborate setting, a dramatic revelation, or climactic event – is complemented by a declamatory gesture or magnified performance. The majority of the actors under scrutiny – Al Pacino, Russell Crowe, Meryl Streep, Michelle Pfeiffer, Daniel Day Lewis – are more than capable of 'big' performances; it is to these films' credit that such largesse is channelled and modulated into more intimate expressions.[5] Conversely, in other moments, the grand scale of an event is held in tension with an austerity or slightness of physical business. In some instances, the fluent course and delivery of many interconnected gestures thread throughout a moment, sequence, and film, gathering significance. Meaning is alternatively sought as the weight of a sustained passage of stillness is punctuated with singular gestures, or moves performed in an interrupted or interrupting rhythm.

The films all achieve a concentration of gesture. Rarely, however, do the works recourse to an easy amplification of gesture through the use of close-up. The magnitude of gestures stems from their integration and adjustment within the surrounding dramatic environment. In *The Insider*, the intense pitch of the men's meetings – as the pressures of media coverage and Big Tobacco's litigious sway mount – is refined by the pattern of gestures accruing within and through the scenarios. The men's cautious relationship develops in physical displays of concealment and disclosure, rigidity and flexibility. Just as Bergman's initial gestures demonstrate an assured capacity for control under constraint, Wigand's introduction reveals a man awkwardly struggling to contain his ranging emotions.

Moving from professional to personal negotiations, *The Bridges of Madison County* is equally alert to the *composure* of gestures. The film explores the concerted containment of feelings expressed in each of Francesca's passing gestures. As the character completes her kitchen chores, each gesture is meaningful in and of itself; the film achieves a greater density of expression in the arrangement and accrual of movements. Tilts of the head and brushes of the hand form a richly textured 'micro-melodrama' of motion and comportment. The housewife's tasks allow for little limited *issues* of frustration. As Francesca finds ways to contain and release her anxieties against the solid trappings of her world, Robert searches, in gestures, to gain a sense of grounding in uncertain situations. The character's physicality couples measures of transience and fixity. Together, the lovers' secret affair forms in an intricate synthesis of tender signs, accruing over the four days and cherished across the years.

Similarly, in *The Age of Innocence* a clandestine relationship forms in brief meetings and seized opportunities, held together by a bond of gestures. The couple create a pattern of coded moves to form an intense private language, concealed under and through public displays of greeting. The substance of each meeting tapers into the hope of securing another. The couple use each moment as a springboard into the next. Caught in these trajectories of desire, Newland and Ellen are unable to appreciate each instant as it presents itself, as it passes.

3

Voice and Conversation

The Age of Innocence

Passing remarks

As noted in the previous chapter, Newland and Ellen's second meeting is brief, coincidental, and seemingly inconsequential. Attention to their words reveals a depth of impact. The chance encounter comes after the prestigious Beaufort Ball (an event marked, for Newland, by Ellen's absence). Taking place on the threshold of the Mingott vestibule, this moment of shared time is seized amidst the chattering comings-and-goings of the characters. While the setting of the opera box held the characters still, caught in a suspended moment, the second meeting shows the couple caught up in a flurry of activity. Ellen and Newland must steal their time together, to create a moment of intimacy within the flow of a social visit. However, within these distinctions, the two separate meetings adhere. The characters find ways to create a sense of continuity through their spells of shared time. They attempt to build up a cohesive relationship through the fragments of their meetings. Such a connection occurs in the form of their conversations.

Each passing encounter only affords the characters the opportunity for a brief exchange. On the Mingott threshold, they deliver a single sentence apiece:

Newland: Of course, you already know about May and me. She scolded me for not telling you at the opera.

Ellen: Of course I know, and I'm so glad. One doesn't tell such news first in a crowd.

Alone, the sentences exist as passing snippets of dialogue. Yet, the form of the characters' words reveals an assertion of continuity, binding this exchange with the moment of their last meeting. The exchange contains no superfluous pleasantries. That the characters get straight to the point reveals an awareness of the restraint constantly placed on their time together. They use each passing encounter to convey their feelings quickly and implicitly. The short lines are compressions of conversation, standing in for lengthier exchanges (denied the couple by circumstance and convention). The stripping away of introductory niceties also gives the lines the sense of Newland immediately taking up the conversation where it left off at the opera. His nonchalant use of 'Of course' reinforces this sense. The sentence sounds like an additional observation, an extra aside to a preceding line. Past and present exchanges connect as parts of a single discussion. This compelling connection takes place within a breezy passing instant, of coats being put on, and people waving goodbye. It is an achievement of the film that this moment appears both casual and deeply consequential. The intensities at play in the brief scene do not announce themselves. The camera seems to catch the instant, rather than charge its focus on significant details. The moment is infused with a palpable sense of the intensity of the occasion, as it passes.

The Insider

Skirting the issue

Finding correspondence with Newland and Ellen in *The Age of Innocence*, Bergman and Wigand cannot move openly and directly to the heart of the matter that binds them. Like the form and expression of their gestures, the two men turn, arch, and twist their words to circumnavigate the legal restrictions. Talking around the issue, in gatherings of hints, paraphrase, tangential chatter, small talk, and *non-sequiturs*, they gradually move towards the truth. Alert to the modulations and adjustments in the ongoing course of the men's exchanges, the film reveals the process of disclosure to be as crucial as the act of discovery.

Invitations and limitations of disclosure

Across the course of the conversations, *The Insider* is sensitive to the particular manner in which information is requested or revealed. To revisit the men's first meeting at the Seelbach hotel, a strategy makes itself manifest in the characters' words, as they offer particular invitations, ways to exchange knowledge. First, as Bergman authorises the spaces of the room with his movements across the floor, he appears to cast wide the parameters of his entreaty to discussion, opening with small-talk: 'Have you always lived in Louisville?'; 'How do you like your coffee, black?'; 'Is there anything you want to know about me?' Yet, the suggestion of polite generality, an encouragement to openness, is tapered as all three phrases form precise entreaties. Bergman's opening chatter comprises carefully tailored appeals, moving increasingly from broad to particular, public to personal (how long have you lived in the city, what is your preference for coffee, what do you want to know about me?). Initiating the meeting, Bergman performs a fine-tuning of polite conversation, offering an open invitation for close expressions of confidence. In his reply, Wigand appears to seal the conversation, even as he opens it up. Matching Bergman's articulate acuity, he offers a question in return. With a sketch of a smirk, he asks, 'How does a radical journalist of *Rampart* magazine end up working for CBS News?' Phrased and delivered as an affront, the question appears as an attempt to block further calls for friendly disclosure. Yet at the same time, Wigand's quip declares his interest in Bergman. Through the defence of sarcasm, Wigand seeks assurance of Lowell's professional integrity, as a necessary test.

Wigand's subsequent words form an invitation of their own, and a call for a particular procedure of disclosure to be set in motion. Scouring the proffered documents, Wigand initially strips his language of any personal colour or signature, hiding behind scientific jargon: 'This is a fire and safety study for Philip Morris; burn rates, ignition propensity, things of this nature.' The technical clarification almost obfuscates a crucial turn of phrase (addressed in Chapter 2): 'That's as far as I go.' Despite the declaration of finality, Wigand is quick to respond to Bergman's question ('As far as you go where?') with more details, elucidating and advancing his situation: 'This issue is a drop in the bucket ... I can talk to you about the issues in this document but I can't talk to you about anything else. I signed a confidentiality agreement. I honour agreements.' In the measure of his remarks, Wigand invites Bergman to seek the truth via a circuitous route of call and response. Again, details are brought out in a precise order: his knowledge of the field (technical jargon); his personal circumstances (the confidentiality agreement); his pride *and* trustworthiness ('I honour agreements'). Wigand is testing the bounds of involvement and implication, setting the game in play.

Voice and position

In a brief and seemingly trivial moment, and in a single stream of words, the film encapsulates the dynamic of the men's ensuing professional relationship. The moment occurs as they meet in a Japanese restaurant. Immediately, the location suggests a precise combination of formality and closeness, felt in the men's relationship at this point. The formal ceremony of Japanese dining is coupled with the intimate arrangement of a table for two. The men sit closely to share food, yet are shackled apart by the confidentiality agreement. Equally, as Bergman learns of the potential impact of the scientist's incendiary findings, his professional interest qualifies the intimacy of his conversation. As the risks and dangers associated with the information become apparent, his concern for Wigand's safety, as a friend, grows stronger.

Turning away from the producer, Wigand directs his attention towards the waitress, to order their meals. He speaks in confident, fluent Japanese. The discussion shows off Wigand's linguistic abilities and articulacy, adding poignancy to his later explanation of his dismissal from Brown and Williamson as being due to 'poor communication skills'. The moment stands in contrast to other, more dramatically prominent scenes in the film, in which Bergman, rather than Wigand, is presented as a powerful controller of serious scenarios (with Hezbollah, covering the moves of the Unabomber). This seemingly minor occurrence, of ordering food, captures the workings of the partnership, testifying to Bergman's wider reliance on Wigand as the carrier of information. As Wigand orders, Bergman must wait patiently to hear what he will receive.

Pitch and tone

As well as creating precise arrangements of dialogue in degrees of disclosure and measures of control, the film is equally alert to the significance of adjustments in pitch and tone, moment to moment.

Two consecutive sequences are considered here. First, the two men's verbal confrontation in front of Wigand's home is seen to bleed together degrees of harshness and softness. Secondly, as the men agree to ride together in the car to the edge of town, a moment of humour inflects and develops a sustained, serious discussion. In fluent modulations of delivery and approach, *The Insider* refines the dramatic density of its dialogue.

Harshness and softness

Before the verbal tirade of the men's confrontation at the Wigands's residence, the film points up an absence of words. The sparse exchanges between Wigand and his wife are designed to speed up their separate departures; sheets of rain divide them further as they stoop under separate umbrellas. The sense of unspoken antagonism heightens, as Bergman appears, silently, in front of the house. Initially avoiding the dispute, Bergman approaches Wigand's wife. Bypassing Wigand, the gesture appears to encourage an immediate diffusion of temper. Suddenly, the politely formal nature of his address to Liane as 'Mrs Wigand' gives way to a gruff aside to Jeff: 'C'mere, I wanna talk to you.' The brusque quality of the words suggests a growing and intense familiarity. It is important to remember that at this point in the film, the men have only met once before. However, their relationship has already passed beyond the superficial niceties and restraints of politesse. Undercurrents of tension encourage certain surges of candour.

Lightness in gravity

As the force of an angry pitch becomes a useful passion, a note of humour encourages the characters' more serious appraisal of their situation. As they move to Wigand's car, to the edge of town, a quip loosens the tension. Again, Wigand appears keen to promote his own interrogation, asking 'What else [do you want to know], outside the zone?' After a beat, Bergman replies 'I don't know. Do you think the Nicks are going to make it to the semi-finals?' Adopting a jocular tone, Bergman risks breaking both the sense of shared conviction, and Wigand's withdrawal. Desperate to find ways to disclose the information within 'the zone', Wigand also appreciates the release afforded by the little joke. The tension of feelings comes out in his facial expression, as he reacts to the remark. Tilting his head away from Bergman, he smiles tersely at the words. The smile quickly turns, his lips pursing.

The joke offers fleeting release, but contains gravity. While creating a momentary diversion from weightier matters, the note of humour emphasises the ludicrousness of the men's position: of having to constantly skirt the matter in hand, to find a way in through tangential topics, to play a prolonged guessing-game. Highlighting the absurd form of their discussions, a moment of lightness and slightness reminds the characters of the magnitude of their predicament.

The Bridges of Madison County

Opening up

In contrast to *The Insider*, in *The Bridges of Madison County*, a move into exposed public spaces encourages a release of words and a possibility for greater intimacy. Francesca's decision to accompany Robert to Roseman Bridge marks a glimpse of a wider world. The retreat from the house opens up a brief holiday from domesticity and everyday commitments. Free from familiar trappings, Francesca airs her thoughts, rediscovering the pleasures and refreshment of new, untravelled routes of conversation. The film first expresses the lightening of a load in two touches. As Robert's truck heads down the track, the photographer asks for directions. Francesca responds, succinctly: 'Out, then right.' The three words, lightly delivered, contain a weight of meaning. For Francesca, once she is out, away from the farm, all will be, may be, right. Heightening the suggestion, Francesca's words are quickly accompanied by a glance by the camera to the mailbox at the end of the drive. A hefty stone is set on top of the box, weighting it into position. Crucially, the view of the load is released just as the truck pulls away, onto the open road.

The film develops the sense of a slow acclimatisation to a more open situation in its handling of the truck's journey towards the bridge, and the faltering conversations of the couple on the way. The act of setting off is marked by a long shot, through the truck's muddy windshield, of the road stretching vertically ahead. Conversation opens up with the road. Surveying the scenery, Robert begins with speculative words, with the breadth of the landscape matching the measure of his remarks:

Robert: Wonderful smell to Iowa, kind of particular to this part of the country, know what I mean?

Francesca: No.
Robert: It's kind of hard to explain ... I guess it's in the loam of the
soil; rich, earthy, alive ... well, maybe not alive. Anyway, you
don't smell it?
Francesca: No, maybe it's because I'm from around here.
Robert: Yeah, I guess so. Smells great though.

The lines introduce Robert's sensitivity to the unfamiliar landscape,
and Francesca's dulled familiarity with the same space, a tension to be
made complex in the couple's negotiation of the bridges. Moreover,
as Francesca's succinct replies appear to close Robert's initiating
remarks, the camera reframes to an extreme long shot of the truck
set amidst the surrounding fields, as it bumps over a stumpy bridge.
Although the scenario is less circumscribed, away from the confines
of the farmhouse, there is an uncertainty to the characters' handling
of their new situation. The wider shot of the landscape expresses
both the capacity for open discussion, and the lacuna within the first
faltering attempt. In an ensuing moment of silence, the passing thud
of the truck bumping onto and off the squat bridge is equally expressive. It marks the gap in the conversation; at the same time it marks
a move forwards, an incremental step of progression. The sound is a
gentle reminder of the act of passage away from the house, and of the
fact that the characters' progress towards the bridge, towards each
other, is being made in stages.

On the journey, the characters' chosen lines of conversation are
expressive of their relationship to their environment. Just as Robert's
remarks encourage an open appreciation of the surroundings,
Francesca's question marks an attempt to fix a person to a particular
place. She asks Robert whether he is 'from Washington originally',
a question that leads to the revelation of his divorce, and so to another
adjustment. The couple share memories of Francesca's hometown in
Bari, Italy. The particular development of the conversation on the open
country road recalls words of Alain de Botton, on journeying:

There is an almost quaint correlation between what is in front of
our eyes and the thoughts we are able to have in our heads: large
thoughts at times requiring large views, new thoughts new places.
Introspective reflections which are liable to stall are helped along
by the flow of the landscape ... the view distracts for a time that

nervous, censorious, practical part of the mind which is inclined
to shut down when it notices something difficult emerging in
consciousness and which runs scared of memories, longings,
introspective or original ideas and prefers instead the administra-
tive and the impersonal.

(2003: 57)

A coupling of large thoughts and views, and precise, shared experience is noted in the film in a repeated shot through the truck's pas-
senger window, bringing together the flowing sight of the fields and
of Robert and Francesca held close, now talking, now huddling to
light their cigarettes. The act of journeying allows the conversation
to broaden, and gives room for introspection; in turn, the characters
begin to find particular points of shared appreciation.

•••

The Age of Innocence presents a world filled with words. The gathered
characters chatter across the film, gossiping in cliques, immersed in
cascades of gracious conversation, streaming from group to group.
At the same time, while awash with words, the world of the aristocracy is exquisitely sensitive to precise turns of phrase. Each remark,
greeting, or response stands as testimony and spoken commitment
to social 'Form'. Each utterance is measured as such; each spoken
misstep is taken as a blow against the speaker. The denizens of this
world are attuned to the devastating power of nuanced expression.
The film forms intricate layers of precise articulation, as the characters speak in public and private, at declamatory pitch or *sotto voce*,
and in the arrangements of the narrator's voice.[1] In a similar manner
to the handling of gesture addressed in the previous chapter, the
film explores Newland and Ellen's attempts to build and sustain a
relationship from snippets of dialogue, to create a coherence of fragments. At the same time, the lovers' hurried words form compressions of conversation, in distillations of private meaning.

The Insider also explores the way its characters shape their words
to overcome surrounding restrictions. Although restrained by the
confidentiality agreement, Bergman and Wigand find ways around
the bind, directing the stream of their words accordingly. The film is
alert to the precise arrangement of each discussion, to how and when

particular pieces of information are revealed, and the shifting dynamic of control to be gained through conversation. A further achievement of the film is the way it shapes lengthy tracts of urgently phrased dialogue to avoid a sense of portentousness. Rather than being tonally burdened as a 'weighty' or 'heavy' drama, *The Insider* retains a sense of gravitas, while it refines its characters' intense conversations in modulations of register, volume, and pitch. The dialogue is rich in depth and density, without appearing onerous or leaden. Free from strain, the words of *The Insider* are still pressing.

Whereas the first two films grade their garrulity, *The Bridges of Madison County* is notable for its paced concentrations of dialogue. Before Robert's arrival, Francesca's life of quiet desperation is marked by attention to duty rather than words. The housewife's few utterances take the form of concise, practical instructions or entreaties: 'Michael, Carolyn, Richard: dinner'; 'Michael, what've I told you about that door?'; 'Would you like to say grace?' Routine direction takes the place of conversation. However, with the family's removal and Robert's appearance, Francesca steps out and finds her voice.

4
Music

The Bridges of Madison County

Refrain, development, and restraint

The film starts without music, without the annunciation of an imposing overture, or the introduction of an instrumental prelude. Yet it is
not in silence. As a close shot of the family mailbox fills the frame,
the sound of field crickets is equally assertive. The susurrations and
rhythms of this natural noise swell and sound across the film, adding to the sense of density developing throughout. Whereas in other
aspects the film achieves a tone of distinction between the 'past'
and 'present' scenes, the blanket of whispered chirrups envelops
both periods, sounding a note of correspondence between mother,
daughter, and son. In the 'past' sequences, the thick zither of wings
adds to the air of quiet suffocation, bleeding together with the hiss
of steam from cooking pans. As the volume of chirruping rises at
certain points, a more promising quality is noted. The sound accompanies Francesca and Robert on their trips to the covered bridges, and
surrounds them as they stroll in the gardens of the Johnson home,
after their first dinner together. A tension arises as the sound wraps
around the characters. The noise is softly stifling; at the same time,
the quiver of wings expresses a nervous awareness of possibility, a
flicker of opportunity, a delicate desire to take flight.

Around and within this cover of natural noise, the film develops a
single musical theme.[1] The decision to limit the musical score in this
way is similar to its handling of space, place, and time. A concentration
on a tightly defined arrangement – of settings, days, and musical

notes – gains a sense of density through patterned returns to the same point. In depth and density, *The Bridges of Madison County* achieves a sense of expansiveness. Through returns to the music, in sounding and re-sounding the same arrangements of notes, the film suffuses the single theme with developing significance. It scores the characters' situations as deeply as the trucks etch grooves in the dusty track to the farm, through repeat visits. The theme also becomes increasingly grand, by degrees, as the narrative progresses: from piano, to strings, to full orchestration. It develops in tune with the nuances of the four-day affair, making adjustments in measures of intensification.

Just as *The Bridges of Madison County* opens without music, it also withholds the score for substantial tracts of time across the narrative. Only when Robert and Francesca huddle together to collect the fallen bouquet of flowers on Roseman Bridge does the film bring in its musical theme for the first time. By introducing the music at just this point, the film underscores the significance of the moment. An initial step, a form of loosening up and coming together, is marked in the release of the first notes. It is a convention of narrative cinema to mark particular moments with music, to signal their importance in terms of plot. In this sense, it is not surprising that *The Bridges of Madison County* chooses this moment to introduce its musical theme. It is in the delicacy of the score's introduction that the film achieves a particular effect: acknowledging the import of the instant and expressing more nuanced forms of development in the characters' relationship. As the trip to the bridge draws to a close, Robert picks Francesca the bunch of wild flowers. Teasingly declaring them poisonous, Francesca causes him to drop the bouquet. All of the surrounding tension, of this unexpected trip and meeting, is released in the little joke, in the falling spray of flowers and Francesca's giddy laughter. Sharing the joke, collecting the fallen flowers, the couple crouch closely together. The introduction of the theme achieves the same lightness as the flowers drifting to the ground. Four piano notes chime. The notes softly build into the key refrain, repeated, adjusted, and developed across the film. A slight and happy moment is quietly marked as the beginning of something bigger. The final repetition of the refrain stops in a minor key. In the sound, the film hints at the tension at the heart of the couple's ensuing and brief affair. In this early event, and in the minor key, there is the suggestion of continuation. Yet the hope for more also contains the promise of completion.

Little developments in the musical theme express crucial shifts in the couple's relationship. The first instance occurs when Robert is invited to dinner. To spruce up, the photographer showers in the backyard. From the bedroom window and behind a gauzy curtain, Francesca cautiously sneaks tentative peeks at the man below. Initially baulking, moving away from the window towards the middle of the room, reproaching herself, she is drawn back, to look again. The film notes the small, pivotal moment of decisiveness in the first repetition of the musical theme. There is a sense of progression, of music and character together. Then, as the piano notes fade away, strings are introduced, separately playing the same refrain. The shift to strings complements Francesca's more confident return to the window and the manner of her gaze; both moves appear a little more pronounced, sustained for a beat longer.

There is one prolonged point of musical assertion. It occurs at the close of the lovers' last shared evening. When his entreaty for Francesca to leave with him is finally denied, Robert turns to leave. As his truck draws away down the drive, Francesca rushes out of the kitchen into the yard. The devastating effect of her decision to stay, and of Robert's departure, is conveyed in the heightened pitch and volume of the musical score, sounded in full orchestration. The only declamatory camera movement of the film intensifies the moment further still. The camera carries with Francesca out of the front door, bumping and jostling speedily down the steps, outside. The instant is amplified not only by pronounced aural and visual points of style, but also by the uniqueness of its fleetingly bombastic rhetoric, within the film as a whole. The heightened register captures the extent of Francesca's silent, climactic sense of hopelessness. For once, tones of disquiet or dissatisfaction inflame into despair.

In the final 'chance' meeting between the lovers (as addressed in Chapter 2), the arrangement of the musical theme carries the resonance of all previous expressions, while marking a moment of irrevocable change. As Francesca notices Robert's presence across the street, piano notes chime to mark the realisation, and a final point of connection. However, in this instance, the musical theme develops around a new variation of the central melody. The notes are the same, but they are played in a different order. It hints at the possibility of change, of Francesca moving to join Robert in the rain. Yet, the 'key change' signals the end of the theme, too. The four days are accompanied by a single refrain; as the refrain changes and disappears, the completion of the affair is sounded in its absence.

Radio days

Alongside the slow-build of the score, *The Bridges of Madison County* textures its soundtrack with a series of radio songs. Jazz and Blues numbers filter into the world of the characters on radios in Francesca's kitchen and Robert's truck. The film is alert to both the intricacies of each song's musical arrangement and its situation in the narrative. Specific musical voices accompany the lovers' affair as it begins, develops, and draws to an end.

The tuning of a radio expresses the characters' attempts to adjust to their surroundings. In the opening sequence of the 'past', Francesca searches for solace in the calm of an aria, before the harmony is broken by the family's entrance and a turn of the radio dial. At the close of the trip to Roseman Bridge, in Robert's truck, Francesca is quick to assist the photographer in his search for 'a station out of Chicago that plays some good Blues'. The shared taste develops the bond of the trip, a gift of flowers, and the savouring of a joke. The song's rhythm and pace also capture the timbre of the moment. As radio and film pick up the song, piano keys bounce, hit with a skit of skimmed drums and the low blow of a saxophone. The springing pace is met by the bound of the 'mean yellow dog' from a neighbouring farm, as it runs alongside the rolling truck. In music and motion, the film builds an energetic sense of momentum. The giddiness inspired by the joke on the bridge spirals into a flighty trip in the truck. Yet, the song's pace also points up the fleeting nature of the visit. As the couple drive back to Francesca's house, the spell may soon break, as humdrum routine returns. The song is taken in like a deep breath of air, as the housewife waits to exhale.

While not selecting and placing the radio songs to demonstratively declare the feelings of the characters, or 'speak' for them, the film allows particular lyrics to be heard at specific points of the narrative. As Francesca extends the meeting with the offer of iced tea, Robert turns the dial on the kitchen radio, finding a little more jazz. A potentially intrusive and impolite act is earned by the fresh confidence of a common interest. The step is forward without being over-assertive, part of a shared pursuit. As Robert sits at the table and Francesca prepares a jug of tea, the radio voice sings 'Now I'm alone with you'.[2] The lines of a romantic standard add resonance to an everyday activity; at the same time, the lyrics continue and give voice to Francesca's unspoken hovering doubt that time spent with this man, alone, is 'wrong'.

While the song acts as a backdrop to the couple's meeting, playing in the background, the film appreciates the particular qualities and intricacies of the music. It combines the variations and improvisations of a piece of jazz with those of the couple's conversation. The radio song gives way to an instrumental break, and the couple sit at the kitchen table, offering polite opening points of discussion, talking about the family. As they speak, the form of their words echoes the shifting phrases of the music, and vice versa. Developing around a central theme, words and music build in changing tones and a staccato flow. Sometimes tentatively, sometimes with assertion, sometimes surprisingly, the delivery of the flow loops and grows:

Robert: Where's your family?
Francesca: My husband took them to the Illinois State Fair; my daughter is entering a prize steer.
Robert: How old?
Francesca: Ah, about a year and a half.
Robert: No, I meant the kids.
Francesca: Oh, Michael is seventeen, and Carolyn is sixteen.
Robert: Well, that's nice, having kids.
Francesca: Yes, well, they're not kids anymore.
Francesca: Of course, being with Richard, so ...
Robert: What's he like?
Francesca: He's very clean.
Robert: Clean?
Francesca: Yes; no, I mean, yes and no. He's other things too. He's very hard working, very caring, honest, gentle, a good father.
Robert: And clean.

Words and music come together. In their misunderstandings, corrections and additions, the couple search to fall in step with each other's tone and direction of conversation. At the same time, on the radio, guitar and trumpet leave and return to the main melody of the song, improvising, finding each other's rhythm and harmony.

Two further moments convey the way song marks the culmination and final faltering of the characters' relationship. In the first instance, in the evening glow of the kitchen, Francesca and Robert dance to the radio as its song billows through the room (see Figure 4.1). This is a crucial moment, bringing the first touch and kiss of the couple. Its significance is emphasised as the pace slows, the camera keeps still in sustained long shot, and the soundtrack is held under the drowsy spell of Johnny Hartman's voice.[3] The complexity of the moment is expressed in the control of volume and pitch. First, the sound of the song moves from the confines of the tinny kitchen radio to bloom in the full expanse of the film's sonic landscape. The shift in sound captures a sense of elation, and the all-embracing rapture of the dance. Bewitched, the couple slowly circle the room. The dreamy quality of the moment is advanced by the sonorous surge of Hartman's low tones. As the depth of bass hypnotises, the quality of the sound also brings out the treble with crystalline clarity. Through its handling of both elements, the film expresses how, while casting a spell, the moment heightens the characters' alertness to their actions. Burning with a smoulder, the instant also sears, carrying the possibilities of consequence.

Figure 4.1   The Bridges of Madison County (Clint Eastwood, 1995): Dancing in the kitchen

The tension comes to a head in 'the Jazz Joint'. Keen to escape the whispering rumours and gossip of the townsfolk, Francesca and Robert head out to a jazz club. Tucked in the corner of the smoky room, the couple appear to find a pocketed space in which they can talk without disturbance. The sound of jazz, of swirling improvised notes, points up the urge to move away from convention and the 'rules' of prescribed order. In answer to Francesca's questions about his past and parents, Robert answers 'I don't know if I can do this you know … to try and cram in a whole lifetime between now and Friday'. As he speaks, the sound of his words hollows into an echo, carrying away in the smoke of the bar and the wash of the music. An echo effect in narrative film often suggests a resonance of memories, and Robert's words chime with his earlier declaration of drinking to 'ancient evenings and distant music'. The ethereality of the visiting photographer catches up with him, and bears the moment, and the affair, into the past.

The Straight Story

Rolling melodies

Whereas *The Bridges of Madison County* develops a single musical refrain into the expansiveness of a full score, *The Straight Story* arranges and combines multiple themes. Within *The Straight Story*, each melodic strand of each musical theme is finely detailed to connect with specific moments of advancement. The compositions intertwine with the development of certain characters, and of Alvin's journey. Musical themes gradually grow to assume wider associations without loosening their intimate connection with protagonists and events. Three main themes emerge within the score. The composer, Angelo Badalamenti, names them as 'Laurens, Iowa', 'Alvin's Theme', and 'Rose's Theme'.[4] The following reading moves through the themes as they are heard in the film. 'Laurens, Iowa' comes first, as the opening and closing music of the film. Next, 'Alvin's Theme' is explored in terms of its interrupted flow throughout *The Straight Story*. Finally, the snowballing effect of 'Rose's Theme' is addressed. Collectively, the significance of each theme is seen and heard to accumulate with each subsequent sounding.

The film begins with 'Laurens, Iowa'. There is a sense of distinction, of prestige, contained in the progressively deepening harmonies of this theme. In sweeping sounds of orchestral music at the start and close of the film, the theme forms majestic bolsters to the narrative. Its twinned appearance encourages the idea of Alvin's journey taking up a small though significant place in a much greater scheme. In this sense, the accompanying images complement the effect of the music. Through the opening and closing shots, the story of the pilgrimage is pressed between corresponding views of infinite space. The grandiose layering of synthesised chords meets with shots of a cosmic, starry sky; a single simple tale is elevated to greater heights.

Other musical arrangements weave throughout the film, from one end of the narrative to the other. The gradual development of 'Alvin's Theme' reflects Alvin's incremental advancement to Lyle. It is first heard at the point of Alvin's departure from Laurens. Much to the consternation of his busybody neighbours, our hero starts his roll down the high street. His theme begins. First, a single guitar insistently plucks out a signature series of ten notes, and again, and again, and again. The repeating phrase forms a bass-line to the music, in each individual sounding of the theme. Alvin's long journey is measured out in little uniform loops of sound. The theme starts to develop, as the sound of a yowling violin joins the dabs of guitar. More sustained notes from the violin are reinforced with a harmonica's wail. The adjustment sets a series of lengthy tones alongside the short, clipped guitar strum. The film establishes an aural equivalent of the long stretch of road carrying consistently spaced short dashed markings. From this moment on, the upbeat folksy twang and chug of 'Alvin's Theme' is bound to points of physical progress. The steady momentum of the musical piece matches the measured advancement of the mower along the road.

The theme shares not only the same pace as the character's moves, but also progresses in the same piecemeal fashion. 'Alvin's Theme' is heard when the protagonist rejoins the main road after a break or pause in the journey. More precisely, the theme is reserved for a small number of instances when Alvin 'kick-starts', rather than merely continues, stretches of his trip. It plays when Alvin returns to Laurens to buy the replacement mower, and as he sets off from his prolonged stay in the Riordan's yard. In limiting the use of the music to these few points, the film subtly expresses Alvin's particular experience. The purchase of a new mower marks the recommencement of the journey from square one. The closeness of Alvin's new friendship with Danny Riordan means that the departure from his house is hard to perform. In marking the culmination of these delays and hesitations, the music sounds out a little moment of straining, of Alvin having to pull away from homely surroundings back onto the road. Perhaps, though, it is also a small fanfare for Alvin, quietly celebrating his resolve.

The film is equally meticulous in its attention to the continuity of the theme through various points of replay. Each consecutive return of the music starts precisely where it previously left off. The first play of the theme is cut abruptly short as a speeding lorry passes Alvin's mower on the highway. As the truck's dash causes Alvin's hat to blow off and the rig to seize up, the musical theme is also left suspended. Alvin is forced to return home. On the point of recuperation, as he climbs aboard his replacement mower several days later, the musical theme is finally heard again and completed. The first notes follow tunefully on from the last notes of the theme's previous airing. The broken development of the theme precisely expresses Alvin's attitude towards his pilgrimage. The music returns as if paused through an interruption. In the pause and resumption of the music, the film conveys a sense of Alvin's resilience, of calmly waiting out the various suspensions of his journey, before continuing on at the point where *he* last left off. It expresses the composure and sustenance of his underlying determination to carry on.

'Rose's Theme' adds a further layer of development, reflecting the growth of meaning from within a quick and seemingly insignificant episode. As this musical theme is gradually established, from collections and repetitions of sounds, the full implication of a small group of images becomes clearer. The theme is first heard as Alvin's daughter Rose (Sissy Spacek) sits at home in the evening, gazing out of the window. From her optical point of view, the camera focuses on a lawn sprinkler. In the same view, a small boy chases after a runaway ball. A cut takes us back to Rose; we watch her watching the boy. The moment appears as a passing fancy, an incidental amusement. Yet, Rose's expression is mute. The music's arrangement develops the curious nature of this fleeting event. Gradually, the sound of slowly plucked guitar strings is joined by that of a languorously bowed violin. The sounds hesitantly develop into a melody. The guitar picks up pace, leading into Latin flourishes, before relinquishing the momentum once again. Tremulous violin strings sound in plaintive waves, rising before fading, disappearing without climax. The tempo appears tentative, searching. Ultimately, it vanishes without resolution.

The tensions in the music reflect the ambivalence of the moment. The way minor tones give way to major; slow cadences to quick; and joyful sounds to melancholia express the quietly conflicting mix of emotions contained in the scene. At this point, the music and the moment coincide to form a niggling question as to the significance of this brief episode, both to Rose and in relation to the rest of the film. *The Straight Story* answers by replaying 'Rose's Theme' at certain points of Alvin's journey. Each time the music is heard, it carries with it the resonance of all previous scenes in which it appeared. Meaning gradually clusters around the theme. It is first revisited during Alvin's campfire conversation with Crystal the hitchhiker. He settles down to tell the tale of Rose's unfortunate past. The musical theme begins to play, and we move to a flashback of Rose watching the boy with the ball. Its meaning starts to clarify. We learn of the death of Rose's son; the news colours the moment of play, and changes our relationship with the fleeting moment. It no longer appears curiously peripheral, and the music's tensions are revealed as containing Rose's sadness alongside Alvin's keen compassion. Just as the theme expresses how Rose's painful memory is tinged with the delight of having the brief opportunity to watch a child at play again, here it also evokes the way that the hitchhiker's sadness moves to more hopeful feelings. Alvin's words inspire the girl to return home to her own family (she is also pregnant). Associations ripple outwards each time the theme is heard, each time it accompanies the activities of another character. This effect occurs as it sounds again, as Alvin later chastises the Olsen twins Harold (Kevin Farley) and Thorvald (John Farley), for bickering while mending his mower. He instructs them that, after all, 'a brother's a brother'. Increasingly, in its placement, 'Rose's Theme' absorbs many inflections of intimate meaning. It becomes associated with all moments of family trouble presented in the film. It reflects the dual senses of discord and harmony found in each particular instance.

Ultimately, this kindred theme reflects Alvin's own concerns about the state of his past, present, and future relationship with his brother. The repetition and development of the theme act as a bridge, an aural track to follow and match the composition of highway travel. It connects the different scenarios as parts of one greater search for familial reconciliation. As Alvin finally meets with Lyle, it sounds again. In this final moment, all the previous connotations of the theme wash together, expressing the eddy of emotions that turns at the point of reconciliation. In its associations and melodies, the theme captures the happiness and regret of lost love.

•••

Contemporary Hollywood's predominant treatment of the musical score connects with its handling of landscape as, to note King again, 'expansive vistas spread out across the big screen' (2000: 1). As the most prominent feature of the sonic landscape, music in contemporary Hollywood is made magnificent in the 'aural impact of multi-channel sound' (1). The high volume of the score meets with the grandiloquence of the musical register. To match the magnitude of the film's visual scale, the musical score is often formed in bombastic movements. Imposing symphonies of sound swell, surround and overwhelm. Whereas the expansive landscapes are used as magnificent backdrops to the business of the film, the musical score asserts mood and meaning, heightening and drawing attention to narrative events. Each significant dramatic or emotional state is keyed by the music, often at a declamatory pitch. In contrast, the two films considered in this chapter find ways to grade and balance their musical scores, to carry inference and resonance. The scores of the two films are not chamber pieces or works of minimalism; they are symphonic works of extended composition, comprising a multitude of orchestral elements. Yet, the music does not blanket or smother the films, or envelop moments in swathes of asserted emotion. Rather, the films achieve a sophisticated variation of dramatic register, through attention to aspects of musical composition.

There are multiple forms of composition in play, and the films hold them in synthesis. First, the written arrangement of the music is at once bold and intricate in design. Secondly, the films achieve an integration of the music with other elements of style. In both forms of composition, the films attend to changing relationships: of key, instrument, rhythm, pace, and tone; of image and sound; between the music and other points of style; through moments; and to characters. Again, the close, significant relationships of style are bound to the close commitments of the characters. The films are also alert to the potential significance carried in the placement and distribution of passages of music. They introduce, develop, and silence pieces of music at precise points. In cycles of chords and motifs, the films create overarching musical themes, forming in union with particular dramatic themes, and developing in concert. Finally, in the films' delicate weighting of these arrangements, the music achieves a further level of composure: sounded without strain, carrying significance without stress.

In *The Bridges of Madison County*, the arrangement of the music echoes the paced concentrations of dialogue. Initially refraining from any musical accompaniment, the film introduces its single theme at exact points and in momentary breaths, expressing measures of release, decisiveness, and resignation. Further, the musical score is complemented by a series of jazz and Blues songs. The collection of voices is heard in harmony and counterpoint with Robert and Francesca's conversations. In *The Straight Story*, multiple musical themes gradually accrue and collect, expanding across the film in precise measure. The points of musical pause and progression echo and express the form of Alvin's journey, and the character's attitude towards his undertaking. A further achievement of the film stems from its handling of the relationship between the development of specific musical themes and motifs, and the changing conditions of the characters.

5
Dissolve and Ellipsis

The Straight Story

Compressions of travelling

In *The Straight Story*, a journey of months compacts into an hour-and-a-half of travelling. As the film shows the road in long shots at precise times, it shortens the way through dissolves and ellipses. Dissolves comprise a slow fade or bleed between two shots, connecting different points in space and time. In ellipses, edits compress long passages of time and cut out periods of journeying. Both stylistic techniques create a condensation of Alvin's pilgrimage. Akin to the particular form and effect of the long shots (as addressed in Chapter 1), the film uses the elements of style to bypass the idea of an onerous voyage over great lands. It chooses not to stress or measure the toll of each step of the journey. Rather, the careful elision and bridging of points express the even restraint and discipline of Alvin's efforts. The tight presentation of the trip, and of experiences along the way, increases the sense of closeness between the individual traveller and the road travelled.

Through a truncation of Alvin's pauses and turns, *The Straight Story* draws attention to road experiences both passing and remarkable. At points, the film cuts to the heart of an episode: the cyclists' passage; crossing the Mississippi by bridge; a graveyard interlude. This concentration pulls into focus the individual essence or spirit of each moment. In savouring the brevity of these passing instances, the film highlights their ephemeral nature and captures their uniqueness. At other points, the film chooses to remove the core of an incident, concentrating instead on the instances surrounding a little event: passing the Grotto as a benchmark; the final meeting with Lyle. In minimising the consummation of a happening, the film reorients attention towards seemingly more negligible moments of passing. It points to the pleasures found in the act of journeying as equivalent to those of arriving. The two forms of ellipses vivify Alvin's time on the road. Each short-lived happening fills the elderly (and ailing) man with brief bursts of vitality. An equivalent joy is felt in neighbouring moments of movement. The film compacts and marries all scenes – those remarkable and those accompanying times – as they arise and pass. In turn, the moments seem to accrue naturally, as part of one distinctive journey.

The film forms clustering miniature versions of prolonged waits and tracts of travel. One striking example of waiting occurs as Alvin shelters from the storm in the roadside barn. Through the wait, we see not only how the storm's passing is carefully compressed, but also how the compression is steadily revealed. The film first lingers on rain-soaked fields, spread in a khaki wash of browns, greens, and greys. The camera pans inchmeal across the wet turf, over to the road. As it reaches the near side of the highway a cut moves to a close shot of Alvin. He is seen settled under the arches, set to watch and patiently wait out the weather. A dissolve combines and passes from Alvin's serene expression into a sweeping view of the revived landscape. Picking up the road at the precise same point of the last long shot's departure, the camera continues the pan, now crossing from the muddy green grassland into fresh yellow crop-fields. The dissolve's slow bleed allows for a subtle transition of time, weather conditions, and the lay of the land. At the same time, it provides a quiet elision of Alvin's stoic delay. In smoothly picking up the road at the exact same point, the camera expresses Alvin's unruffled readiness to continue; the pause has not set him off course. Changing states of the countryside connect with and through Alvin. A close-up of the character mediates the shift from weatherworn to sunny. Corresponding colours encourage a sense of integration. The dark green of the trailer's tarpaulin tones with that of the sodden grass. The burnt crimson of Alvin's jacket meets with the wheat's glowing amber. As well as tightly entwining visions of man and landscape, the dissolve expresses a gradual spreading of warmth, of and for the way ahead.

As with the pause, joined points of progress tell little stories of adjustment and change. The effect alters with the journey's turns, moving from Alvin's passage along the road to connections of disparate locations. As well as abbreviating the mower's slow crawl over long distances, a delicate ellipse and bleed of dissolves capture particular rhythms of travel. One such instance occurs just prior to the barn's appearance. A tight series of shots conveys the mower's passage over the highway's hilly contours. Rather than repeatedly show the rig rising and falling with the road, the film encapsulates a sense of recurring passage in a single dissolve. Three shots capture a rhythmic move over 'that [hill] and two hundred just like it.' The brief arrangement of angles and shapes conveys the mower's ongoing negotiations of the route. Contrasting diagonal lines suggest the steep upturn and decline of uniform dips in the road. The dissolve bleeds the lines; in the space of the bleed, the mower's wheel is seen to cross and cut through the long stretch of tarmac. The shots express the achievement of a little goal, of successfully tackling the hillock. The clash of contrasting diagonal lines suggests a passing stroke of toil; it is a jounce of road and rig and yet, a moment later, sensation and knoll are overcome. At the same time, the crosshatch also points to Alvin effortlessly 'cutting across' swathes of distance, calmly embracing the whole journey, rather than worrying over regular obstacles.

In a few rare instances, the film turns its attention from Alvin to consider occurrences elsewhere. In the buffering of a dissolve, a brief glimpse of other places inflects the experience of Alvin's ongoing journey. Such a moment occurs on the point of the character's initial departure from his home in Laurens. The mower sets off, tight to the road's edge. In a dissolve, the long shot merges with a closer view of two farm machines at work in the field. The camera slowly moves around the rigs; a further dissolve returns focus to the road. Alvin has made some progress; a previous scattering of houses and onlookers has been replaced by open stretches of farmland. The dissolves' slow bleeds create a cushioned transition. The road's gritty tarmac texture melts into willowy gusts of reeds. A smoky waft of crop-dust adds a further filter to the dissolve's fusion. The act of embarking on the trip is marked gently, pleasing in its gentleness. It also feels *right*: Alvin's fit with the land is snug; his place there is found without fuss.

In the shapes, textures and dissolve of two long shots, the film also points up affinities in Alvin's venture and the harvesters' range. Both locations harbour two mechanical rigs moving people across the land. Alvin's trailer is coupled to the mower; the harvesting machines are linked by a metal arm. As the wheels of Alvin's rig turn in tandem, the harvesters work together to keep adjacent, sharing pace. The connection suggests the vehicles and drivers as part of a greater whole, comfortably accommodating each other in tasks of quiet toil. Like the harvesters, Alvin now relies on the land to provide support. Instead of marking difference, the film's moves between distinct locations and events create cohesion. Alvin is placed as one of many parts, connected to countrymen and landscape alike. Further, the move to the other vehicles continues a sense of Alvin's gradual progress, carrying in the harvesters' own slow mechanical rotations. The film enhances the sensation in the camera's continuous cycle around the rigs. Shot and wheels turn together. The dissolve establishes a rhythm of movement not only shared by harvester and mower, but also wholly created within the moment of their juxtaposition. Tracing over the land with the harvesters, Alvin progressively reaps his own rewards. The move through the moment suggests how he quickly reverts to the slow cadence of a natural cycle, taking instinctive steps back to his brother.

One further example shows how *The Straight Story* uses dissolves to explore defining moments of separation and togetherness. The moment merges two different times and locations. In pairing instances of departure, a passing mix of images expresses the complexity of Alvin's feelings about the pilgrimage. When the mower breaks down on the road, Alvin is forced to return to Laurens and start his journey again. A dissolve joins the character collecting his replacement rig from Tom 'the John Deere dealer' (Everett McGill) with a view of Rose waving him goodbye. In the dissolve, the film elides Alvin's return to the house. It passes over any discussions between Rose and her father, choosing not to show Alvin's renewed preparations for departure. On the surface, both the ellipse and Alvin's movements appear easily achieved. In the mower park, his leave-taking occurs in a clipped manner. He departs in and amidst neat straight lines: right to left of yard and frame, up and out. An upright window strut in the middle of the frame bolsters the sense of the moment's straightforward architecture: straight lines, decent dealings, direct exit. Yet, a sense of reticence marks Alvin's subsequent removal from his daughter. The camera withdraws more slowly from Rose, arcing around her in a last lingering curl.

The film creates a pang of upset in the dissolve between events. As the different spaces bleed together, the dividing window bar of Tom's office appears to separate Alvin from Rose (see Figure 5.1). The father, in one place, is simultaneously connected with and set apart from his daughter in another. The dissolve creates a subtle, fleeting impression of how Alvin will miss Rose out on the road. While eliding the painful protraction of returning home, readying oneself for the road, long goodbyes, the bleed of the dissolve lets a little anxiety leak out. Yet, the sorrow of temporary distance and comfort of lasting closeness intertwine. Rather than show a dejected Rose pine for her father (and vice versa) alternately to emphasise their isolation from each other, the film uses the dissolve to bring them together even in separation. While leaving Rose is painful, the image suspends the daughter in anticipation of Alvin's return.

The Age of Innocence

Elisions of a lifetime

The scattered, passionate meetings of Newland and Ellen are encompassed by the broader circumstances of Society life. Yet, the surrounding New York affairs share aspects with the lovers' brief rendezvous.

Figure 5.1   *The Straight Story* (David Lynch, 1999): Alvin missing Rose, missing Alvin

Each enveloping scenario is presented in a particular form of compression. At points, extensive periods condense into passing moments. At others, the film trims and bridges individual happenings in a High Society 'Event', measuring even the slightest occurrences of the elite world. As a result, all events surrounding the lovers' meetings take the form of compact vignettes.

The film condenses each episode with ellipses and dissolves. As the ellipses of *The Straight Story* compact an extensive journey, those of *The Age of Innocence* mark and concentrate specific stages of the characters' lives. There is a further important distinction. *The Straight Story* is particularly interested in the transitory images that form in the middle of an eliding dissolve. The attention of *The Age of Innocence* focuses on the moments surrounding the ellipses. These peripheral points, of passing words and gestures, stand in for the details absented in the elision. They do duty for the 'unsaid' and 'unseen'. At the same time, they draw attention to the omissions, emphasising what is left out of the aristocracy's colourful histories.

Following this distinction, there are two interrelated ways in which *The Age of Innocence* creates ellipses of events: as those within and those acting for a happening. As a basic division, the ellipses within events are expressed visually – in dissolves and camera movements – whereas the ellipses around events are marked verbally, in passages of dialogue. (As will be shown, the differences in the designs of both strands are more fine-grained that this primary distinction allows.) Through ellipses within events, the film presents distinct episodes and occasions in varying measures of extensiveness. Although all Society occasions are compressed into individual vignettes, some occupy a greater part of the narrative than others do. The Beaufort Ball is detailed in meticulous measure. Conversely, the wedding of Newland and May is encapsulated in a few brief dissolves. The film alters the magnitude of its ellipses within events to grade the significance of certain occasions for the members of this society, and for individual characters.

At other times, the film removes the 'core' of an event entirely. The fact of a particular happening is marked by its elision. The missing detail of the event is replaced with inference and suggestion. Instead of witnessing a set of circumstances, characters and viewer alike hear about it in passing snippets of dialogue. Although the philandering Beaufort is rarely seen, whispered accounts of his affairs (past and present) marble the film. Equally, both Newland and viewer are denied direct intelligence of the true tone of May's 'wonderful talks' with Ellen. Instead, the content of these crucial little meetings is trimmed into May's innocuous recounting to Newland.[1] The details of Ellen's personal history scatter through the film. They come piecemeal as snatches of gossip, and from disparate sources. Likewise, the shifting particulars of her divorce seep into the narrative, through a fragmented series of meetings between the barrister Letterblair, Newland, and the Countess herself. The true measure of her relationship with the Count's secretary (Monsieur Rivière) is never ascertained, remaining instead as a confusion of rumours and glances.

In creating ellipses of and around the core of particular affairs, the film shows how the characters' lives are filled with intimation, circumscribed by murmurs of suspicion. As the film's narrator marks, the characters belong to a society in which, 'the real thing was never said or done or even thought', a world 'balanced so precariously that its harmony could be shattered by a whisper.' Indeed, it is precisely the fragility of the society that promotes a desire to keep all potentially damaging 'un-pleasantries' hidden, denied, or better still, completely eradicated. As Ellen plaintively demands of Newland as they sit together in her apartment, 'Does no-one here want to know the truth …?' Altogether, through ellipses around events, the film shows how this insular society preserves itself by maintaining a vacuum at the centre of its affairs.

The focus of my reading, however, will be on the first strand of ellipses, on those composing and compressing the body of an event. The form of ellipses within events can be seen to vary significantly. In each case, the film encapsulates an individual episode or period. It maintains a sense of the whole of each event (each dinner, concert and ball), while abridging the time taken for the occasion to pass. At the same time, the particular meaning of each event is expressed through a particular use of ellipses. Three key grades of compression can be noted, together with corresponding instances to be analysed further. First, at certain points, the film creates tiny compressions of time, eliding mere minutes or seconds of a passing action. It chooses to present the Duke of St Austrey Dinner in this way. Second, on other occasions, the film uses ellipses to convey the evanescence of a single, extended event. Both the wedding and honeymoon of Newland and May are presented accordingly. Finally, in its penultimate sequence, the film compacts many years of Newland's life into a single unbroken movement of dissolves. Differences in the amount of time compressed (seconds, minutes, days, years) couple with correspondingly distinct styles of compression.

To mark the occasion of the Duke of St Austrey Dinner, the film marries repeated ellipses of tiny increments of time with a focus on minutiae. The course of the dinner itself is shaped by multiple dissolving views of ornate articles, set out for the guests to admire. Throughout the event, the attention of the camera is on the *objets* and paraphernalia of 'grand entertaining', not on the guests themselves. In turn, the significance of the occasion for the characters is refracted through this close study of trappings. Primarily, the steady focus and magnification of little delicate objects makes a prominent point to guests and viewer alike. As Joy L. Davis remarks of this scenario, 'Crystal, china, centrepieces, silverware advertise their [the Van der Luydens'] affluence, their cultural heritage, and their aesthetic taste' (1993: 466). Further, the scrutiny allows the camera to obsess over the objects, as the people of this world would do.

The film then deepens the effect in its style of movement through the views. As well as magnifying the articles, the camera pans slowly over them, as if traversing a meticulously crafted landscape. Moreover, while maintaining a fluid pan over the objects, the film condenses its perusal into a series of dissolves. A graceful passing view of one decorative plate or bowl bleeds into another. Through the dissolving moves, the film captures a particular manner of scrutiny. In abstract form, it conveys the way the guests of this elite event might survey the scene. In the smoothness of its close passes over the ornate pieces, the camera performs an intense yet apparently casual inspection of items. In bleeding together views of small clusters of articles, the film expresses the sense of someone 'taking it all in, all at once', while noting, in passing, individual details.

At the same time, the design of the camera's moves highlights the careful arrangement of the objects themselves. The passing views follow a precise rhythm, with the camera repeatedly moving from right to left over one piece, then left to right over the next. Each move is synchronised with the passing of each dissolve. A remark by V. F. Perkins on the precise rhythms of *The Magnificent Ambersons* is particularly pertinent. Perkins observes that, '[the camera movement's] unhurried fluidity enhances the sumptuousness of the display'

(1990: 46). The observation is equally applicable here, as the refinement of each edit and move matches the elegance of the pieces exhibited, and the form of their exhibition.

There are more complexities in the moves. In *The Age of Innocence*, the careful patterning of views suggests an all-encompassing sense of order. The regular pace of each dissolve to the next piece matches the symmetry of each move. The film measures out the entire dinner in this fashion, passing through close dissolves of crystal and china to flowers and food. The rigid structure of the moves is held in tension with their easy grace. As such, there is a mechanical modishness to the movements. With each dissolve, the film shows how, for the aristocracy, each movement is bound by a strict ordinance of rituals and routines.

Even the slightest act is imbued with a governing sense of ceremony. As dinner is served, the camera continues its fluent appraisal of the event. It attends to the fine detail of the food. Each dish has the same ornate elegance as the trinkets on display. The camera focuses momentarily on a meticulously presented platter of whole salmon. Through a series of dissolves, the film traces the serving of the dish from platter to individual plate. The action takes the form of a 'momentary ceremonial'.[2] It is a fleeting moment, fluidly presented in the camera's continuous glide and through the dissolves' bleed. Yet, this trifling act is performed with great procedure. The food is seen to with fastidious care by the serving staff. The camera's trace matches the waiter's precise and dignified moves. The little ceremony matches the symmetrical patterning of moves across the objects, passing right to left, left to right. In turn, the rhythms of this minor act, of the serving of one dish, feed into the flow of the dinner as a whole.

The act's mechanical grace conceals a crucial omission. A dissolve elides the waiter's task of skinning the fish prior to service. In its place, the film bleeds in an intermediary view of another dish, of a pretty plate of prepared oysters. It offers a momentary diversion before dissolving back to the dressed fish. The miniscule, seemingly inconsequential elision carries a significant resonance. In the dissolve and ellipsis, the film removes the 'vulgar' sight of the skinning. The elision is barely noticeable, as the moment carries through in a rhythmic passage. An 'unsightly' incident goes unseen. For the members of this elite group, all activities considered ungainly, trivial or momentous, are elided. Through the ellipsis of a passing moment, the film shows how the mechanical grace of rituals and routines absorbs 'un-pleasantries' with absolute ease.

The occasion of Newland's marriage to May is presented with similar automatic refinement. Again, the film uses a careful patterning of dissolves and ellipses to compress a grand Society event, measuring its ceremonious form. In this instance, the compact views become more intimately inflected, and reflect a personal detachment. An arrangement of ellipses expresses Newland's overview of the occasion. Whereas each moment spent with Ellen appears enchantingly prolonged, his wedding to May is quickly passed over, marked in a matter of minutes. The film's brief treatment of the event makes it appear as a glancing disturbance in the order of things, not as a benchmark occasion. The elliptical views form more of a contraction than a concentration.

Both wedding and honeymoon are presented as lifeless occurrences. They are marked in a dissolving flow through fixed tableaux. The film bleeds together views of the wedding gifts – glasses, silverware – as the narrator recounts the bare-bones facts of the day. In turn, the honeymoon – an extended trip to Europe – is compressed into a passing series of painted vistas. In both instances, fleeting images of *objets d'art* replace views of the newlyweds themselves. Equally, the presence of the guests and well-wishers remains invisible, or rather, is represented by the gifts. For the honeymoon, all human activity is sketched onto canvas, as static illustrations. Throughout the sequence, people are substituted by things, by a series of tokens. While noting the overwhelming importance of such trappings for this society, the film appears to strip the wedding of human involvement. The only activity of the inert scene comes from the camera's movement over the fixed compositions, and the passing dissolves through the views. The procedure of social ceremony – the wedding day, the honeymoon – is marked by, reduced to, the mechanical process of the film's own movements.

At the same time, the particular nature of each automated movement can be seen to express a form of human influence. Primarily, the influence of the aristocracy as a collective can be detected, as guiding the *form* of the couple's matrimonial business. Marking the honeymoon, the camera's rhythmic tracing of painted scenes (from top to bottom, left to right) recalls its strictly ordered moves at the Duke's Dinner. In this instance, the patterned movements are carried out as the narrator dictates a set schedule, of how the couple travel to 'all the expected places'. Accordingly, the film skips through a series of impersonal painted snapshots of London and Paris: Westminster, the National Gallery, the Tuileries Garden. The tight order of camera moves matches a brisk stepping-through of the 'expected' locales. Altogether, there is a sense of the pre-ordained, of Society's government of the couple's every dealing. Convention and tradition strip the occasion of individual personality, reducing it to a series of required moves.[3] The use of dissolves heightens the sense of the couple being effortlessly guided in prearranged ways through the event.

If we are to understand the sequence as infused with Newland's own sensibility, then these mechanical rhythms of compression can also be seen as particularly expressive of his passage through proceedings. In this brief episode, the film marries a sense of Newland being 'carried through' the wedding by prescribed measures with marks of emotional distance. On one level, the camera's course over the surface of things, of gifts and canvas, conveys Newland's superficial investment in the occasion. Equally, the tight order of moves expresses, in abstract form, a sense of Newland 'going through the motions'. Camera and character move in step and with pliancy through a set pattern of events.

In the sequence's closing moments, a final ellipsis suggests how Newland similarly sleepwalks through an extended period of his marriage. The couple are presented in close-up, in the honeymoon carriage. Gradually, from the frame's far sides, the image blacks out, pushing inwards (see Figure 5.2). The movement (together with the narrator's elegiac phrasing) gives the scene a sense of closure. Shutters are being softly drawn on the honeymoon. Newland's tentative hold on events loosens entirely. It is as if both Newland and the film drift into sleep. Yet, the sense of closure is short-lived, the slumber interrupted. After a moment's pause, the scene reawakens. The black shutters of the fade open again. The characters are once more seen sitting side by side in the carriage. However, within the fade's sleepy wink, the film compresses the first six months of Newland's marriage to May. Compared to the iridescence of moments spent with Ellen, this period is so vapid for Newland that is disappears, in the fug of a doze. Through the sequence, to the last ellipsis, the film expresses

Figure 5.2   The Age of Innocence (Martin Scorsese, 1993): A marriage fades

Newland's indifference to the passage of his life with May. Ultimately, he submits himself to eddying turns of the social 'Season', allowing procedure to carry him. (A further, white fade engulfs the scene, carrying the couple forward in time to May's triumphant performance at the Archery Club.) The hollowness of Newland's experience is as much marked by the eclipsed moments between events, as it is by the evanescence of the occasions themselves.

Towards the end of the film, however, one moment with May is made piercingly alive for Newland. Any remaining hope of his to rekindle a relationship with Ellen is definitively snuffed out as May announces her pregnancy. In an instant, Newland is locked into his life in New York. His vision of the world, previously filled with images of Japan and plans to travel, suddenly contracts. You feel he can see the remaining years of his life spanning in front of him, heretofore complete.[4] The film combines all of these sensations in one fluid movement. Even before the news is allowed time to sink in, the camera arcs away from Newland, around the room. Again, this man is being carried along in eddies of governing circumstance. This time, with all the prospects of seeing Ellen again now gone, his submission is absolute. Eddies collect into a single slow swirl of passing time. Decades of Newland's life now quickly dissolve in the unbroken arc of the circling camera. The portrait of his personal history reduces to a single vignette of a solitary room. As the camera continually traces around the chamber, the sense of entrapment, of 'going nowhere, going round in circles' is starkly expressed.

The affairs of Newland's family life also appear to contract into this one small space. As the narrator observes, 'It was the room in which most of the real things of his life had happened.' Through ellipses, significant events compress: the christening of Newland's eldest son Ted; the announcement of his daughter May's engagement; her wedding day. Through dissolves, the events reduce to glimpses of defining gestures: the baptism of the child; embraces between May and Mary, Newland and Mary. Each glimpsed event, although significant, appears intangible. The camera's continuous revolution and rhythmic flow of dissolves disallow a prolonged marking of events. As soon as it is witnessed, each event ebbs into the governing flow of motion. Momentous occasions are seen in passing, passed over.

This sense of impalpability extends to views of the room itself. Through a gradual progression of ellipses, the room's aspect alters by degrees. From the middle, the camera traces smoothly over walls and furnishings. Through dissolves, the style of particular objects – table lamps, a desk chair – changes with the period. The alterations are moderate, yet collectively transformative. Altogether, the film creates a continuously shifting sketch of the room, redesigning itself through the years. As a result, this solid place, filled with a lifelong collection of personal mementos – the sculpture of May's hands; the photograph of her archery triumph – is presented in a constant state of flux. The established and fixed parts of Newland's life are also insubstantial, uncertain.

Displacement deepens in the measure of each dissolve. The film inverts the expected relationship between the amount of time elided and the amount of space covered in a dissolve. In this sequence, the more fractional a move, the more extensive the temporal period covered. Instead of an inchmeal movement between two points conveying the ellipsis of a few seconds (as in the Duke's Dinner), here it compresses many years of Newland's history. The dissolve is almost imperceptible. The camera passes slowly across Newland's desk. In the move, the image of the desk chair bleeds into a more modern design. In the space of the bleed, the film seamlessly connects together the moment of Ted's christening with the announcement of May's engagement.

Conversely, a more prolonged and discernible dissolve is performed without the elision of any time at all. For Ted's baptism, the camera strokes past the assembled group of Newland, family, and priest. A lap dissolve moves through views of the wetting of the baby's head. Yet, the move does not condense the moment, or connect it immediately with a future event. The dissolve fragments the sight of the baptism as it takes place, as if parts of the picture softly slide away from each other in passing. In troubling the association between the amount of time and space covered in a dissolve, the film expresses Newland's floating displacement from the events of his world.

Throughout the compact scene, the camera traces the room's circumference from a fixed central position. In turn, the 'real things' of Newland's life are performed against a mercurial backdrop of changing surfaces. Events and objects shift together to form a tableau, moving continuously across the enclosing walls. The centre of the room remains unseen. From this perspective, the film encapsulates the hollowness of life with May, as devoid of a core. Ellen's absence creates a lack at the centre of Newland's being. In this brief moment, his later life reduces to a series of ephemeral images, encompassing a void.

•••

Dissolves allow for a breaking-up and passing-through of images in film; ellipses enact omissions. In narrative cinema, the devices are used to truncate measures of time and space, eradicating 'dead moments' and connecting disparate events, periods or locations. The handling of the two elements in *The Straight Story* and *The Age of Innocence* holds true to these principles of compression; yet equally here the use of dissolves and ellipses provides more than a means of truncation and transition. In the decisions that go into the making of these two films, even the more abstract or non-figurative points of style express precise measures of human closeness. In both films, dissolves and ellipses develop a conveyance of shifts in the characters' moods, circumstances, and relationships.

In *The Straight Story*, an extensive period of travelling is compacted; in *The Age of Innocence*, lifetimes are surveyed in abridged form. The flow of these long dramatic courses carries in exact undulations. In some instances, by dissolve or ellipsis, an apparently minor happening is heightened in an intensity of feeling or incidence. In others, the act of compression conceals or reduces a moment's bearing. On occasion, fleeting events encapsulate the characters' wider circumstances. The two films pay particular attention to patterns emerging in compressions, of colour, texture, and shape. In both works, the process of measurement is keyed closely to expressions of the characters' attitude and experience. Dissolves and ellipses convey grades of weariness, sorrow, and pleasure that suddenly emerge or accrue over time.

Alvin's travels are compressed as measured pleasures of process and progress. In particular, spontaneous and passing events are expressed and appreciated as momentary. Conversely, *The Age of Innocence* is alert to the way New York aristocracy constructs each 'Event' as a significant happening. As each dinner and Ball is shaped through meticulous attention to 'Form', any intrusive element of potential unpleasantness is instantly elided or closed over. In dissolves and ellipses, the film measures the impact of each social ceremony on Newland and Ellen. Passing instances gain in private measures of intensity for the couple; prolonged periods apart become empty, hollowed out.

6

Position and Perspective

Drawing together the concerns of the book, this final chapter reaches back to considerations of place and patterning, to extend thoughts on the way that camera and character negotiate their wider environments. As Chapter 1 considers the films' shaping of panoramic vistas and patterning of settings, this section attends to aspects of viewpoint and focus, on the way particular details are brought out across the breadth and width of the surroundings. It concentrates on the films' channels of attention. The terms 'position' and 'perspective' here refer to the different ways a film's camera and character are situated in, and make sense of, different environments. The camera's placement, in distance and angle, offers graded perspectives on a film's events. The precise changing position of the characters is equally significant, as they move and look around landscapes and locales. The shifting relationship between camera and character adds a further level of meaning. At times, they may share a viewpoint, in the film's alignment of angles, patterns of looks, or use of optical point of view (POV). At others, the camera's perspective on an event may contrast, in degrees, with the character's position.

The Age of Innocence

Focusing in

In measuring Newland and Ellen's fragments of shared time, the film creates an elaborate panorama in passing acts. As each moment plays out, the camera catches at details. The film immediately introduces this way of seeing in the opening sequence at the opera. It presents an overture of brief views. Moment by moment, it harmonises glimpses of grand assembly, of the setting's designs (the opera house) and the characters' congress (the opera audience). The viewpoint changes constantly: moving from extreme close-up to long shot and back again, sliding together diminutive and expansive arrangements. As the camera strokes over passing features, they collect: a yellow chrysanthemum plucked on-stage; Newland's buttonhole snowy rose; a row of white lights; the glimmer of an earring; a chain of uniformly trussed men. There is a pointillist synchrony in the composure of views; it is suggestive of the way the opera-goers take in their surroundings to get the measure of their neighbours: roaming across the setting, seizing on details, making connections.

The sense heightens as the camera assumes the viewpoint of 'New York's foremost authority on "Form"', Larry Lefferts.[1] Lefferts and camera scrutinise the assembled crowds through the lens of opera eyeglasses. The view of the scene tapers to that of one discerning figure, through the narrow scope of the lorgnettes. Yet, the idea of discrimination (from an authority on Form) is complicated as the film initially holds off from an impression of concentration. As camera and glasses pass over the regimentally amassed gathering, the scene remains a nebulous whole. Passing views of the grand room fan together. The camera flutters over the scene as Lefferts searches for a focal point. Glints and shards of detail appear, yet the whole vista remains in a swirl. Scorsese offers a pertinent observation here:

> When you look through binoculars in a place like that, it's almost like a kaleidoscope of images that hits you; you see so many things on the periphery of your eyes.
>
> (Smith 1998: 74)

The idea of 'things on the periphery of [one's] eyes' is crucial to the sequence, and to the film. In this early instance, the film expresses and combines distinct meanings of 'the peripheral'. Through the view offered by the opera glasses, the entire scenario appears as a fanned collection of opaque images. Lefferts searches these surface views for something to pin down and critique in piercing wit. Each glint and gesture caught in the kaleidoscope offers the promise of salacious interpretation. For members of the elite, the actuality of grand events such as the opera is of scant interest. Rather, each occasion contains a kernel of opportunity to scrutinise the behaviour of clans.

Within a constant flurry of fleeting details, the film creates moments of fixity, of focusing in. Ultimately, Lefferts's keen scrutiny is rewarded in the sight of Countess Olenska taking her seat in the Wellands' private box. Her opalescent blue dress and the twinkle of her lorgnettes in the stage-light draw his hungry attention. The roaming gaze fixes on the new arrival. The film simultaneously captures the fresh fervour of Lefferts's look and the irradiance of Ellen's appearance. Responding to a sudden concentration of focus, the camera now holds still over Ellen settling herself into the box. Aghast, Lefferts baulks at the Wellands' audacity. Now, what will Newland do?

Moments of 'focusing in' capture acts that are private but also open to public detection. In particular, the film uses lighting effects to encompass and illuminate peripheral activities. Two trips taken by Newland provide good examples: first, alone, to the flower shop; then, with the rest of the grand families, to see 'The Shaughraun' at the opera. In the first example, the sequence opens in long shot, Newland walking down the street in full view. As the camera monitors the scene from on high, there is the suggestion that even the most apparently incidental act is observed, surreptitiously yet studiously, in this community. In the darkness of the street, a warm yellow glow of roses smoulders in the window of a flower shop. The sunny dash of colour attracts Newland, causing him to pause in his stride. As he turns to face the shopfront, the camera arcs smoothly around, slowly drawing towards him. The use of an iris focuses on his movement to the shop door and his entry (see Figure 6.1). As the iris draws in, it captures the precarious balance of tautening feelings. Risks of public exposure and personal intensity encircle the act, which concludes with Newland sending yellow roses to Ellen anonymously.

A bolder iris effect accompanies a daring claim to intimacy when Newland and Ellen attempt to steal a moment at the opera, at the performance of 'The Shaughraun'. Like the earlier opera meeting, discussed in Chapter 2, the scene conveys the intense mix of emotions forming and fading in a brief period. As the curtain falls on Act 1 of 'The Shaughraun', the film focuses, with Newland, who is seated in the stalls, on the activity in the Beauforts' opera box. Beckoned

Figure 6.1 *The Age of Innocence* (Martin Scorsese, 1993): Iris in the flower shop

by Mrs Beaufort from her seat above, Newland enters. The box contains Countess Olenska and leading figures of this closed coterie: the Beauforts, Sillerton Jackson (Alec McCowen), Larry Lefferts. As Newland crosses to sit with Ellen, the camera moves left to a frontal view of the box and then adjusts right to follow Newland's movement; as he sits the iris encircles the couple, while simultaneously shrouding the other characters in darkness (see Figure 6.2).

Meeting the concentration of the lighting, the film tapers the soundtrack. Initially, on Newland's entry, the sound of chatter from the opera box forms an intricate web of voices: Beaufort exchanging 'pleasantries', Mrs Welland gossiping with Sillerton Jackson. As Newland shifts his attention to Ellen, the light condenses, and so too does the soundtrack. The ambient sound and the conversation of the other characters in the box recedes, leaving the voices of Ellen and Newland exposed. The turn of each word is magnified, each note of inflection amplified. Others critics have marked the intense use of light and sound in this brief moment. Dessun Howe notes how the iris effect leaves 'the two aspiring lovers in an isolated circle of intimacy' (1993). Equally, Amy Taubin reflects on the precise tapering of voices, with the film 'rising in on the lovers and then dropping out the sound, so it seems that for each of them nothing else exists for the other' (1999: 9). Yet, previous attention does not address the way *The Age of Innocence* sustains a sense of the couple's exposure, alongside that of their intense connection.

Figure 6.2   The Age of Innocence (Martin Scorsese, 1993): A night at the opera

Ellen, alluding to the action of the play, asks Newland 'Do you think her lover will send her a box of yellow roses tomorrow morning?' There is a complex sense of magnification. Image and sound enact the couple's intimacy, though the use of the iris within a continuation of the wider shot, together with the focusing of sound, creates as illusory the couple's aspiration to privacy in the social space of the box. The iris casts other characters into the shadows, but Mrs Beaufort remains close by. Maintaining the artificially restricted sound, a closer succession of two-shots visually excludes the other nearby characters and intensifies the emotional significance of the couple's exchange. The precise timing of the cut, coinciding with Ellen's first words here to Newland, conveys the total absorption of the lovers in each other. Yet, it is crucial to note that the film first, subtly, marks out the presence of other characters alongside the couple. Each exclusive moment is qualified by a suspicion of discovery.

The seal of this 'isolated circle of intimacy' is ultimately, inevitably, broken. Newland blunders a response to Ellen's finely weighted question:

Ellen: And what do you do while May is away?
Newland: I do my work.

An awareness of the presence of the neighbouring characters, though now unseen, appears to shape Newland's flat reply. In turn, the impersonal remark shifts the tone of the moment. Ellen is crestfallen. The film conveys the change in Ellen's demeanour through subtle alterations in the circle of lighting. It reaches the nuances of a transitory moment through a deft handling of the event's diegetic lighting effects. That is to say, it balances the emotional course of the lovers' encounter with the rise and fall of the stage-lights (of a theatrical production). In turn, the grades of the theatre's lighting precisely match the changing situation in the box.

The transition in the 'periphery event' of Newland's meeting is met by developments in the public 'Event' of the operatic play. As Newland responds to Ellen, the audience lights are dimmed, and spotlights stream down onto the stage for Act 2. The change removes the circle of light from around the couple, as Newland's reprimand is heard. Further, the move forms a searing arc of white light behind Ellen alone (see Figure 6.3). This flare of light heralds a new tone, and a distinct, intense moment of implicit reproach: 'I do want you to know what you advised me was right. Things can be *so* difficult sometimes, and I'm *so* grateful.' With these whispered words, Ellen reaches for the lorgnettes, and gazes intently down towards the activity on-stage, away from Newland. The focus on their meeting is eradicated. The play's orchestral score soars up once more, engulfing the scene. The meeting between the lovers has formed an intense interlude. Acts of the play form bookends to the private encounter. In fixing the meeting under the spotlights, the film draws into focus a deeply personal moment entirely inflected by surrounding circumstances.

Figure 6.3   *The Age of Innocence* (Martin Scorsese, 1993): A quick flare-up

Camerawork and lighting combine as *The Age of Innocence* weaves an intricate crosshatch of looks. Describing the opening sequence, Leslie Stern observes a 'choreographing of looks between members of the [opera] audience' (1995: 223). Similarly, and using the moment to remark on the mechanisms of New York Society as a whole, A. Robert Lee notes:

> This, indelibly, as, alongside, we see through the binoculars to Ellen and her Mingott-Archer clan, is a world of gaze and predatory watchfulness, and in which any deviation from the norm implies not only risk, gossip, but, at worst, removal from sight, or, as in Ellen's case, seemingly complete erasure.
>
> (2000: 171)

This network of looks feeds into the film's texture of flurrying activity and glimpsed detail. Lee describes the elite as constantly surveying each event for the slightest inconsistency. Finding such a glint of interest, Society is seen to fix quickly upon it. The film occasionally suspends its passing flow over events and occasions to fix upon the gaze of an individual character. At points, the character looks directly into the camera, intensifying the sense of an interruption or puncturing of events. In these moments, the direct gaze of a character into the camera creates a concentrated centre of attention. As with the iris, the film is able to form an acute point of focus while retaining sight of surrounding circumstances. Some instances happen within a public social occasion (such as the Beaufort Ball); others occur when characters read private letters.

The sequence of the Beaufort Ball begins with a shot of the dark and empty ballroom as the narrator introduces us to the Beauforts' somewhat compromised social standing. The chandelier's lights come on, dancers materialise in the image and a succession of shots displays the formality of their massed ranks in the splendidly illuminated ballroom. Rows of white gloves on a table lead us to Newland's entrance and the camera moves with him in a complex and elegant long take through the drawing rooms; the camera sometimes leaves Newland to view paintings as he passes them, but keeps pace with his leisurely movement through the house. The narrator comments on the house and its contents, and offers us perspectives on Newland Archer's relationship to this intricately rule-governed and highly conventional society. Cutting away from Newland, the camera now weaves among the dancers and groups of guests while the narrator offers ironic insights about the significant players in New York Society as they are picked out. We lose sight of Newland. As the narrator mentions May Welland, the camera comes upon a group of young women and May fixes the lens with a crystalline gaze and beaming smile. Instantly, the bearing of the moment alters. Whereas camera and viewer previously enjoy a detached appraisal of each guest, May's direct gaze exposes the presence of this roaming onlooker, the camera's status magically transformed and identified in this moment with Newland's point of view. A responding reverse shot shows Newland returning a fixed gaze and smile. He must yield his wandering eye; his attention tapers only to May. Matching 'direct to camera' looks sharply lock the characters together. As the narrator observes at that moment, 'May Welland represented for Newland all that was best in their world, all that he honoured, and she anchored him to it.'

The film narrows and secures the anchoring effect to Newland, Ellen and May. It also further refines the effect by establishing a particular approach in a pattern of moments. It chooses to fix upon the eyes of the trio as they narrate passages of their letters to and from each other. As the characters study the notes, we hear their voices reading the words on the page. This distinctive technique, of direct looks and an oblique form of direct address, expresses a complex tension of intimacy and exposure. Looking directly into the lens, the characters confide thoughts and reveal personal decisions: to marry, to travel. Through these private missives, they disclose feelings and intentions, away from the 'world of gaze and predatory watchfulness'. Yet equally, the particular pieces of news contained in the letters are meant to be interpreted not only as personal confidences but also as public statements of intent. As the characters air their written thoughts, there is a declarative edge to the delivery.

Each delivery's meaning comes in combinations of direct looks and address. Four examples from across the film can be considered. First, a crucial moment of physical intimacy between Newland and Ellen is interrupted by a message from May. In Ellen's private apartment, the lovers break their embrace (through a dissolve) as a servant enters, carrying a letter on a silver salver. After reading the letter,

Ellen passes it to Newland. As she does so, the film moves to a sight of May, chirruping with delight at her news:

Ellen,
Granny's telegram was successful! Grandma and Mama agreed to marriage after Easter! Only a month!! I will telegraph Newland. I'm too happy for words and love you dearly! Your grateful cousin,
May

As well as interrupting a passionate moment, the news has wider implications for the couple, rupturing their relationship. The sense of the letter acting as a fissure to the situation is intensified through the immediate contrast in colour between the two scenarios. Ellen's quarters are cast in dark, warm tones, offering close shelter. Conversely, May 'delivers' her message in the open air. She is set against a backdrop spray of bright flowers, matching her dainty pink bonnet and the fizz of her words. Her giddy brightness sears into Ellen's shaded retreat. In holding back the piercing vision until Newland reads the message, the film emphasises the impact of May's news on her husband-to-be. Equally, in doing so, it replaces a view of Newland's reaction with one of May gazing directly into the camera. As the camera slowly draws into her fixed stare, the look engulfs everything else.

In a further instance, the film omits the precursory view of a character receiving and reading a letter. It moves straight to the sight and sound of the writers themselves, as the message is being read. This occurs as Ellen 'delivers' a letter to Newland from the Van der Luyden's country retreat. In focusing directly on Ellen, the film conveys the immediate impact on Newland. It expresses the letter's unexpectedness and force. (The message instantly reorients Newland's plans, as he rushes to meet Ellen at the Skuytercliff house.) At the same time, the film shapes the moment to explore how Newland's reading of the letter infuses the vision of Ellen as she 'delivers' it. His emotional reaction to the words inflects the way she speaks the letter aloud. Her delivery takes the form of spoken verse, as the words trip by in a skipping meter:

Newland, I
Ran away
The day after I saw you at the play.

> These kind people have taken me in; I
> Wanted to be quiet and
> Think things over.

In Ellen's lyrical performance of her words, the film suggests how, for Newland, the message forms an incantatory invitation. Accordingly, he sets off for the Skuytercliff house. Crucially however, the film shapes the moment, using Ellen's 'to-camera' gaze, to trouble the association with Newland. Initially and in long shot, Ellen appears to be looking directly into the lens, as she recites her words. However, as the camera draws ever nearer to her, it becomes apparent that Ellen's eyes are fixed marginally aside, into the distance (see Figure 6.4). Her gaze does not quite meet the camera. The match is fractionally misaligned. In an instant, the misalignment offsets the intense personality of her words to Newland. The moment of imagined intimacy is subtly worried by the film's precisely discordant use of a fixed look. Existing only in the mind's eye, a private fantasy remains incomplete, *out of true*.

A third example forms a point of excoriating intensity for Newland and a revision of previous instances. It comes after an (unseen) 'incidental' tête-à-tête at Mrs Mingott's house, in which the seemingly ingenuous May has secretly revealed the news of her pregnancy to Ellen. (This news is still, at this stage, unknown to Newland.) The news prompts Ellen to write Newland a cryptically formal letter, informing him of her decision to return to Europe. The following

Figure 6.4   *The Age of Innocence* (Martin Scorsese, 1993): Ellen looks askance

day, after leaving the opera early, Newland stands with May in their drawing room, on the cusp of confessing his love for Ellen. Seizing the moment, May silences Newland, presenting him with the letter telling of Ellen's imminent departure from the country.

Immediately, the film marks the particular momentousness of this letter for Newland. It creates a distinct variation of its approach to similar moments. The focus in this instance is on the reader (Newland) and not the sender (Ellen). When the letter is presented to Newland by May, the camera moves in to scrutinise Newland's reaction. At the same time, the two gas lamps on either side of the fireplace magically dim; in place of naturalistic lighting, an intense beam tapers on Newland's eyes (see Figure 6.5). For this character, at this point, the rest of his world falls away, replaced by an absorption in the letter. In an act of fierce concentration, light and words burn into his eyes. The effect balances opposing aspects. While expressing the intensity of Newland's focus on the devastating news, the light also hints at Newland's awareness of the possibility of May's direct glance; in turn, it highlights May's respectful (yet calculating) propriety in pointedly not looking at him as he reads. As Newland begins to read, the film draws together the sound of his internal voice and Ellen's echoing recital (she is unseen, but heard). The film also distils the soundtrack to the two lovers' voices. Crucially, Newland's voice bookends the delivery of Ellen's words. Before her tones are heard, Newland *intones* her words as he reads. Their voices

Figure 6.5   The Age of Innocence (Martin Scorsese, 1993): Newland has news

momentarily fold together. As with the poetic incantation of the previous example, a message from Ellen is infused with Newland's own perception of the occasion. This effect reaches its melancholy conclusion in his final chimerical vision of Ellen, at the end of the film.

In the closing moments, the film concentrates all that has gone before into a final act of 'focusing in'. All of Newland's shards of time with Ellen condense and reduce to one shaped memory. In a fleeting moment, the film expresses Newland's desire to 'deal all at once with the packed regrets and stifled memories of an inarticulate lifetime' (Wharton 1948: 360). It occurs as Newland stands in front of Ellen's Paris apartment, as he withdraws from present hesitations into his acute vision of the past. Spatially, the film narrows the setting to the corner of a small square, off a busy boulevard. It keeps the camera close to Newland, looking down on the now elderly figure, or up to the high windows of the apartment building, searching wistfully for Ellen's quarters. Both camera and character finally focus their attention on a single balcony. As Newland's son Ted (Robert Sean Leonard) decides, Ellen's window 'must be the one with the awnings'. Newland dispatches his son up to the Countess with a message to explain his non-appearance ('Just tell her I'm old-fashioned; that should be enough').

Again, the film trains a single beam of light on the character's eyes, to suggest the intense concentration of the man and the moment. Newland settles on the bench, fixing his gaze on the window above. As he does so, a glint of sunlight refracts off the window's edge. The rays fill the screen, sending Newland into his reverie of Ellen (see Figure 6.6). As the window shuts, sunlight and vision fade away. Newland stands to leave the square. The musical score and a flock of birds soar up together, forming a brief crescendo, before settling again. In the reverie, Newland fixes on one particular memory of Ellen, as she stands at the water's edge in Newport. Adrian Martin describes the vision as a 'theatre of memory'. He continues:

> Newland gets to replay, in his mind, and at last put right, the moment that once upon a time stymied him for the rest of his long and uneventful life. He wished for the Countess Olenska ... to turn around before that Murnau-like boat passed and, if so, all would be well with the world, and between them as lovers. It

Figure 6.6   The Age of Innocence (Martin Scorsese, 1993): Newland's flimsy, filmy dream

didn't happen then, and now it happens with tremendous yearning but no joy.

(2000)

The singular exquisite vision is a *re*vision. It is composed of all of Newland's 'tremendous yearning' not only to immerse himself again in this small yet all-encompassing part of his life, but also to reshape it according to his desires. A. Robert Lee describes the vision as the encapsulation of 'another world':

> The film, here, too, acts scrupulously on the novel's suggestion of Ellen's life and its passage as enclosed in another world, 'this rich atmosphere', but which, for Archer, finally remains best to be seen only in imagination.

(2000: 173)

Lee raises a crucial point, observing that Newland would prefer to retreat into a fantastical reverie than see Ellen 'in the flesh' and in the present. The film emphasises this choice, showing Newland turning away from the window with the force of the light, squeezing his eyes shut to fix on the image in his mind. (Newland's gesture may well be matched by the viewer's own reaction, as the intense light fills the screen, encouraging fleeting recoil.) The act also echoes Newland's declaration to Ellen at the performance of 'The Shaughraun'. Having watched the curtain fall on the electrifying end to Act 1, he confesses, 'I normally leave the theatre at this point in order to take the picture away with me.'[2] Now there is nothing stopping him from seeing Ellen, he again turns away.

Despite the intensity of Newland's purpose and desire, to revive and reshape a memory as the 'composite vision of all he had missed' (Wharton 1948: 360), the attempt is hopelessly futile. As Martin notes, 'it happens with tremendous yearning *but no joy* [emphasis added]'. There is no sense of elation found in the endeavour. Newland's past relationship is irredeemable, and certainly, in a flight of fancy, irreparable. The film conveys the pathos and emptiness of Newland's last vision in a number of ways. Most immediately, the image is shown as a fantasy. The deep pink sky and shimmering blue sea suggest a heightened state of perception, with the image filtering through as part of an intoxicated dream. At the same time, the vision comprises the final sliver of Newland's fragmentary moments with Ellen. It forms a flimsy compression of all their shards of shared time. Again and for the last time, Newland attempts to fix their moments together with a sense of intransigence. The translucence of his final concentrated vision only highlights the impotence of the attempt. Moreover, it stands as testimony to the *virtual* nature of Newland's entire relationship with Ellen. The film heightens the sense of simulation, revealing the image *as* an image. In foregrounding the 'filmed-ness' of the image, it points up the fancifulness of Newland's vision. The imagined moment of Ellen's turn is presented as a projection, playing only for Newland, irrupting into the actual world of a Paris street. As V. F. Perkins notes more broadly, 'Movements through time and space that are not absorbed into the "and-next-ness" of storytelling will necessarily draw attention to constructedness, to artifice and the artificer' (1990: 41). *The Age of Innocence* promotes this sense of 'artifice' by laying bare the surface textures of Newland's filmic reverie. The image is seen as a series of superficial layers, of matte backgrounds and plastic details. It is overtly presented as a photographic trace, a flimsy film of a memory. The blatancy of expression exposes the emptiness of Newland's vision. It reveals a lack of true substance.

In the final frames of the fantasy, the film recalls the mismatched direct look of Ellen's address to Newland at the Skuytercliff house. In this instance, the eyes of the dreamed and the dreamer fail to meet;

Figure 6.7   The Age of Innocence (Martin Scorsese, 1993): The true heart of the film?

the eye-lines do not match. Again, the desired intimacy of the connection is lost, and the hopelessness of Newland's attempt to join with Ellen, in this way, is compounded.

Perhaps the true heart of *The Age of Innocence* lies elsewhere. In a passing glimpse, quickly subsumed by the more colourful affairs of Society life, the film provides an image of complete kinship, of the sort Newland desperately attempts to find in his reverie. As Newland collects Ellen from the train station, an elderly couple emerge from the swirls of platform smoke (see Figure 6.7). For a beat, they fix the camera with a stare, arm in arm, before the fog gathers around them again, and the film's attention moves on to the awaiting carriage. In a glancing moment, the film presents a vaporous vision of Newland and Ellen's impossible, unattainable future. The old couple pass as ghosts, but the fixity of their gaze impresses itself as the memory of an impossible prospect.

The Straight Story

Events momentary and momentous

The Straight Story's handling of focal points allows it to combine two significant characteristics. The film displays brief instances that are experienced as fleeting. Equally, certain passing actions appear as momentous, as holding an enduring sense of importance for their participants. Throughout Alvin's journey, the film repeatedly presents individual moments in this tension. It builds a series of sequences that explores the short-lived but long-felt sensations coexisting in particular moments of life. If certain parts of the film are visited with this idea in mind, then three separate and inter-related groupings are seen to emerge. The three are: (a) extensive periods of waiting and travelling compressed into momentary spells; (b) long-awaited moments fleetingly dealt with as passing events; (c) seemingly incidental moments gradually revealed as greatly significant.

The most extensive case in point for group (a) is that of the con-densation of a month-long journey into a two-hour film. In group (b) the film quickly passes over incidents of apparent consequence. For example, the locale of the Grotto is repeatedly referred to by many of the characters, along different stretches of Alvin's journey. It is seen as something of a local benchmark, as a significant place that divides different parts of the region ('you must live north of the Grotto'). As such, it is set up as a momentous marker along Alvin's route to Lyle. His passing the Grotto suggests the crossing of a certain point, the reaching of a milestone. Yet, it receives nothing more than a passing glance by the film. As Alvin approaches the landmark, the camera remains tight to the side of the mower. Neither lens nor character lingers by the monument. The film quietly notes the fact of its presence and Alvin continues down the road. Rather than a denial of the landmark's importance to the traveller, the fluid move past the Grotto allows for an unobtrusive acknowledgment. True to the nature of this particular traveller, a moment of importance is quickly felt, accepted, and absorbed. The significance of the instant rolls into the journey's greater meaning.

My reading focuses most on the third type of grouping. In group (c), the film pays close attention to seemingly insignificant moments. Two instances are exemplary here: Alvin's crossing of the bridge over the Mississippi, and his encounter with a group of cyclists. Alvin's experience of crossing the river comes in an intricate patterning of optical point-of-view shots. Moving onto the bridge, character and camera look up to see its towering metal struts set against a marbled blue sky. Up and then down: the griddled surface of the bridge's base skims under the rolling wheels of the mower. A glance to the right reveals a small town on the river's far bank. The film locks into a personally oriented experience, a rush of shifting views. Each optical point-of-view shot couples with a close-up of the character's facial expression. Subtle measures of pleasure wrinkle across his mouth and eyes. These are fragments of views, as oblique in their brevity as they are private in their appeal.

As the passage progresses, Alvin's appreciation of the experience meets another turning point, bringing a sense of unease. When character and camera look down the length of the bridge to the other side, the musical soundtrack breaks from the rhythmic harmonies of Alvin's theme into one, low, held chord. The sinister rumble of the note matches a change in Alvin's eyes: harmony gives way to apprehension. He blinks, refocuses, furrows his brow. There is a sense of Alvin 'coming to' from the distractions offered by the elevated viewpoint of the bridge. As he fixes his eyes on the gradually encroaching bank, the crossing's broader implications seem to draw nearer too. Through two dissolves, the film widens the inference, bleeding from man to bridge to the next pit-stop setting of the graveyard. Moving through the views, the film softly suggests the reason behind Alvin's moment of perturbation. Is he too late to reach Lyle alive? It is in keeping with the film and character's worldview that such a dreadful worry is not expressed as a daunting revelation, but as a passing shudder.

Throughout Alvin's moves across the bridge, *The Straight Story* explores aspects of suspension. Primarily, the scene contains a literal sense of suspension, of a bridge carrying Alvin over the depths of the Mississippi. In itself, this fact adds a slight edge of precariousness to the event. Alvin is shown redressing the swerves of the mower, constantly having to 'right' himself. Further, as the use of optical point of view isolates particular features of the bridge, there is a suggestion that Alvin is trying to savour the moment. As the mower rolls on, the character's attention is drawn to certain characteristics of the bridge as they pass him by. The length of the point-of-view shots and the returns to Alvin's face express a sense of delight in detail; moving across the water, he 'drinks in' cursory sights. From suspension to distension, fragmentary points of focus pull the moment apart. The measure and number of passing views appear to extend the little crossing and stretches of appreciation. Alvin attempts to dwell on the bridge's features, to grasp at passing aspects. At the same time, in fracturing views, the film notes how it is precisely the fleetingness of the sights that sustains Alvin's sense of pleasure.

An unusual achievement of the sequence stems from more distanced views of the bridge inflecting and conveying Alvin's experience. Between views of the bridge's metal top and base, the film cuts to a wider shot of Alvin astride his mower. Alvin is shown as one part of a broader scenario: of bridge, sky, and land. In opening out into a wider vista between circumscribed point-of-view shots, the expansive sight is pocketed into personal views. A lesser film might easily have introduced the scenario through immediate recourse to grand designs: of an extreme long shot of the bridge stretching horizontally across the extent of the frame. *The Straight Story* gives us this anticipated shot, but does not start the sequence with such an overly dramatic move. It first moves through a careful arrangement of views linked to Alvin's position. When the extreme long shot comes, it marks a turning point in Alvin's experience: he is now more than half way over the Mississippi; the long-promised moment of crossing this bridge is now passing; he is nearly with Lyle. A moment of wider appraisal, of taking the longer view, briefly allows for a more detached outlook.

There are similar designs at work in Alvin's later encounter with the cyclists. Yet, whereas Alvin anticipated the pass over the bridge, a sudden surge of cyclists is entirely unexpected. The film folds together aspects of swiftness and surprise. A jolt comes first, reinforced by prior moments of dawdling and stillness. The instance occurs after Alvin's sedate stop-over in the barn. It is preceded by a leisurely set of movements over the regular curves of the landscape. As the camera ambles to accompany the mower's slow progression along the road, a blurry bright-coloured man-sized shape flits past. Others follow in quick succession. Alvin's surprise stems from the speed of the darting riders' abrupt appearance (and disappearance). The sudden arrival of a vast group of cyclists on a farmland track has an incongruity that increases the bewilderment.

Through its choice of focus at this juncture, the film ensures that the cyclists' passage is as surprising for the viewer as it is for Alvin. It keeps the camera trained on the mower in static close shot. The angle prevents the viewer from any foresight of the cyclists, as they approach Alvin from the distance. The initial flit past the mower and across the frame constitutes our first sight of the riders. At the same time, in focusing on the mower as the cyclists begin to pass by, the film asserts Alvin's position within the moment, as it happens.

As the first rider rushes by, a shot change carries a flinch. It is a little jump, a little jump cut. The cut comes in the middle of the cyclist's pass by the mower; it forms a 'crease' in the continuity of the rider's movement. Ever so slightly, as Alvin blenches, the experience joggles. Camera and character are taken back apace.

As with the Mississippi crossing, the film channels into Alvin's experience ever more tightly, moving into point of view shots. In this instance, the move to Alvin's optical point of view also conveys a crucial change in his attitude towards the moment. Shock quickly turns to pleasure. In a tight series of views, the camera whips to follow individual cycles as they pass. The swift turn is also that of Alvin's head, pivoting in pace with the riders' dash. The shots express Alvin's satisfaction in the hurtling instant, in a *heady rush* of vitality. Each turn of his head matches each whooshing movement onwards by a rider; Alvin advances his involvement in the moment. He finds a way to keep up, and to be caught up.

Again, a move from optical point of view to wider shots expresses a development (rather than detachment) of Alvin's intimate experience. Following tight and speedy views of the riders skimming by the mower, the film opens up. A long straight line of cycles in motion stretches up the road. The progression of different views of the cyclists shows how Alvin gets to grips with a surprise encounter, altering his bearing to best effect. First, he involves himself in the instant, catching at views of individual riders. Next, he allows himself to reflect on the scope of the situation, catching his breath. In a jigsaw of different perspectives, the film suggests how Alvin works to get the most out of the event, to puzzle it through.

As if responding to Alvin's completed reasoning of the instant, the film moves on, out and up. Unlocking itself from the character's optical point of view, the camera cranes from the mower's side in a fluid rise. Settling high above the road, it tilts down on Alvin and cyclists below. A cut takes us higher still, to a bird's eye view of grey track and yellow fields. Stretching horizontally across the frame, the road's chalky strip is peppered with a line of tiny figures. The cyclists move in a swarm from right to left in uniform progression. Just as the riders' arrival buoys up Alvin, here they appear as ants, as if carrying the mower as a prize morsel back home (see Figure 6.8). The camera's rise gradually introduces a different sensation of a fleeting moment. As seen from high above, the cyclists' progress appears to

Figure 6.8   *The Straight Story* (David Lynch, 1999): Ants on a track

slow. A distant perspective draws out the landscape and stretches the instant, ending Alvin's *weighing up*. The cyclists' swarm forms another momentary distension, an encounter to savour, yet always as part of a bigger picture. When Alvin catches up with the cyclists at their lodgings, he tells them that 'the worst part of being old is remembering when you were young'. The chance meeting has been bittersweet, offering a tension and distension of feeling. This elderly man enjoys the quick rush and longstanding melancholy to be found in a passing blast of youthful energy.

The Bridges of Madison County

On and around the bridges

Like the previous film, *The Bridges of Madison County* focuses on the setting of a bridge to explore positions adopted and suspensions enacted by people at certain times of their life. The transient nature of the setting, as an intermediary place between places, matches and promotes the transitory relationship of Robert and Francesca. The conclusion of their time together is undetermined, up in the air. In the trips to the bridges, the lovers are held between points, between progressing and saying goodbye. Equally, echoing *The Age of Innocence*, the film explores a couple's attempts to fix images of each other in a series of meetings, to make them fast. The two characters visit the bridges together twice over the course of their four-day affair. Francesca's accompaniment of Robert on the first trip, to

Roseman Bridge, is a spontaneous decision, breathlessly performed. Her second visit, to Holliwell Bridge, is in answer to Robert's invitation, hence marked by readiness and anticipation.

The first trip: Roseman Bridge

The film is particularly adept at exploring the way the characters approach the bridges and each other. An unfamiliar approach to a fixed setting allows for the possibility of change. Robert comes as a stranger to the presence of the bridges. They are well known to Francesca, yet the accompaniment of this outsider to these local landmarks encourages the housewife to see them anew. Robert's unfamiliarity allows space for curiosity, placing expectations on hold, and permitting observations of bridge and photographer alike. As a photo-journalist, Robert seeks to find the most evocative and striking angle from which to capture the setting. In turn, this professional process encourages Francesca to look afresh at the bridge, while developing a keen interest in the man. Robert's meticulous way of seeing contributes to Francesca's enthusiasm and guides her to be more conscious of feelings – of both bridge and man – that she might otherwise have experienced only partially or hurriedly. Both characters search for the most appropriate positions to view, and from which to be viewed. They look to find stances of assurance, moving apart to come together.

Before the characters find separate standpoints on Roseman Bridge, the film details a shared approach. As discussed in Chapter 1, the fixity of a particular locale (in that instance, the Johnson house) is pointed up in a series of movements towards and away from the setting. The act of the characters reaching their destination is marked first in a series of long tracking shots, of the truck on the road, then in a close vertical view held stock still above the truck, of the path stretching and curling towards the bridge. The sense of arrival is expressed in a tightening of focus and a lock of attention. Equally, the move from tracking shot to static view highlights the rigidity of the setting, a fixed look at a fixed design. The bridge is being presented as a set place to be approached, ready to be explored and appreciated. The concentration of attention is also felt in the tight framing of the couple's heads through the truck's rear window. In their initial sight of the first bridge, Robert and Francesca are of the same view.

Perhaps as is inevitable in new friendships, the sustaining of an immediately synchronised view of the world is a fragile affair. As the characters get out of the truck they become physically separated, their outlook divided. The sense of necessary separateness develops from an initial hint, sounded as a neighbour's car crosses the bridge on the couple's arrival. A car horn toot of friendly recognition fractures the couple's shared appreciation of the view, alerting Francesca to an alternative perspective of the situation, of how she may be viewed by others. As her hands flit to her face, they mark Francesca's desire to be held from view; in turn, the gesture momentarily draws her away from Robert. A shift in position is promoted as the film cuts in opposing angles of the now stationary vehicle. The intrusion of the neighbour's greeting has altered the bearing of the moment.

Stepping from the confines of the cabin, the couple are set apart by the open container of the truck's hold. Against the hold, their sense of the situation is marked as separate. For Robert, the spirit of the moment has turned from anticipation and open conversation to purposeful activity. Clutching his camera, his movement out of the truck is marked with nimble business (addressed in Chapter 2). Reaching into the container, he flips open his work-bag and lifts out the tripod. In contrast, for Francesca, the arrival to the bridge continues a sense of irresolution, of open possibility. Exposure and a lack of grounding carry in the sounds accompanying Francesca's alighting. As she steps outside the truck, the air is thick with the chirruping of crickets. There is restlessness in the noise, and a sense of fragility, of slight delicate friction. Amidst the sustained, low zither of wings, a single quick snap of the tripod marks Robert's move away from Francesca, towards the bridge.

Suggestions of separateness develop in attention to levels and angles. *The Bridges of Madison County* places the protagonists on different planes. Searching for the right angle from which to capture his view of Roseman Bridge, Robert heads purposefully down the slant of a neighbouring knoll. The move allows him to gain a fresh sense of perspective, to experiment with angles, to hone his vision. It also sets him further apart from Francesca, who lingers uncertainly by the bridge's mouth. As the distinct positions break the characters' shared perspective, they express Francesca's sense of removal, away from Robert's more involved appraisal of his circumstances. At the same time, the distance affords Francesca an opportunity to study Robert, unobserved, for the first time. Her position on top of the bridge offers her a vantage point, while also setting her at the periphery of Robert's trained gaze. As the photographer negotiates different views of the bridge, Francesca tries out a range of positions from which to watch the man below. Both search for the best perspective.

The couple are also set apart in differing levels of direction. Robert's assured course is held in tension with Francesca's fretful situation. There is a smooth fluency to Robert's stride and motions; although new to the locale he is at ease in this environment, a state hinted at in the way his khaki shirt melds with the tawny scrubland. While the photographer experiments with different angles, there is a sense of sure conviction in his steady placement of the tripod: setting it down on the grass, affixing the camera, training his eye to the lens. Placed at the base of the mound, Robert shows a willingness to immerse himself in the landscape, to approach his subject at ground level. Contrastingly, Francesca struggles to find her feet, making tentative circling steps atop the hill and bridge. She is uncertain of how to place herself in this setting; the situation and locale inspire a sense of dislocation. As the colours of Robert's shirt blend easily with the scenery, the starched whiteness of Francesca's dress is set against the cornfield's bright yellows and greens. At the same time, the pallid material matches that of the fences abutting the bridge. There is a suggestion that through her negotiations, Francesca may find a position of support in this setting.

Closeness tentatively grows as Francesca seeks sanctuary in the bridge. Walking hesitantly towards the wide wooden mouth, Francesca allows herself to steal glimpses back at the photographer, emboldened by the promise of refuge and retreat. In moving under the cover of the sheltering arches, Francesca places herself in Robert's sightline. A stride towards concealment contains an act of declaration. As the progression inside the bridge gives a meandering moment a sense of direction, Francesca moves in step with Robert's view. While placing herself in the picture, she tucks her frame against the side of the bridge (see Figure 6.9). Again, this character draws strength from the solid support of a fixed structure. Her body is held snug against the wooden divider, her white dress matching the wall's wash. In a moment of repositioning, Francesca aligns herself with the setting. Her shifting standpoint affords a different perspective; from a secure site of cover she can steal glances of her new companion.

Figure 6.9 The Bridges of Madison County (Clint Eastwood, 1995): Suspended in thought

For Francesca, the growing mystery of an unfamiliar man is marked out in a view from the bridge. Peeping out and down, camera and character catch a glimpse of the newcomer below. The sight of Robert is framed on either side by the white slats and struts of the bridge's barriers, forming a fractured triangle of slanting lines. The oblique aspect of the view captures Francesca's sense of the day's peculiarity, of being at odds with herself in the presence of a stranger. While her spying suggests a desire to see more, her view of Robert remains, as yet, tantalisingly restricted.

As in *The Age of Innocence*, a fixed image of another person is only an ephemeral achievement, shifting and reshaping with the passing moment. The hold of Francesca's gaze is first troubled, and then released, by the distracting flutter of a bird's wings, sounding from the shadows of the bridge. The flap of feathers points up Francesca's nervousness, but also an increasing hint of excitement, of the character opening up to distractions and diversions. All fixed resolutions are placed on hold, suspended on the bridge. One distraction from daily duties, of Robert's unforeseen arrival, leads to other smaller interludes. While drawing her attention shortly from the man below, the noise of the bird stirs Francesca to a further appreciation of her surroundings. With a flutter of wings and heart, she is moved to touch the textures of the bridge walls, to draw further into its dark enclaves. In the shadowy hollow of this place, the nature of things remains uncertain, unclear. Moving further into the bridge and the afternoon, Francesca is charmed by the promise of possibility.

The inner structure of the bridge compliments the housewife's private designs. Tracing her hands along the wooden slats, Francesca comes to the middle of the bridge. An involved arrangement of crisscrossing timbers forms chinks and peepholes, allowing the character to continue her pattern of stolen glances below. As the film cuts quickly between two close shots of Francesca stooping to sneak a peek, it captures the stealthy breathlessness of the gesture. The closeness and brevity of the shots is held in contrast with a long lingering view of the photographer, in an expanse of grassland. Francesca's cheeky undercover glances give way to an image of openness. The declarative nature of the shot befits the moment, as Robert calls up to Francesca, 'Always this hot around here?' In the assertion of voice and view, the film confirms Robert's acknowledgment of Francesca's presence. Within an act of open announcement, there is the suggested recognition of her clandestine attempts at watching him. The sense of exposure develops and transfers to Francesca in a further shift of perspective, as the film cuts to the first, and only, shot of the housewife on the bridge from Robert's point of view. The singularity of the view points up the sense of revelation. Fixed in long shot, framed in a peephole, Francesca has been caught out. For the first time, both characters turn their attention to each other, and acknowledge their efforts.

The kindling associations of the sequence progress in measures of distraction and attention, restraint and release. Having been 'caught out', Francesca looks to recover her composure. With a quick answer to Robert's query, she turns away from the barrier, withdrawing into the shadows. A further flutter of wings accentuates the note of agitation, and matches Francesca's fretful dabs of her hands to her face. Suddenly, her silent questioning of an uncertain moment is answered in a further call from Robert. The photographer invites Francesca to take a soda from the truck. For the housewife, this familiar call for provision releases her from the charge of the moment. She seizes the invitation, moving away from the more exotic possibilities gathering in the space of the enclave. With a raised hand and a flick of the waist, Francesca looks to redirect the course of the afternoon.

Running to the truck and reaching for the soda, she cools down, quenching her thirst. An opportunity for release is contained within a moment of control.

The retreat inspires a further turnaround. Drawing deeply on the soda bottle, Francesca swings back in the direction of the bridge. The loosening of tension afforded by a return for refreshment is troubled in a moment of disorientation. Robert's presence is suddenly marked by his absence, and by the new positioning of his camera and tripod in the mouth of the bridge (see Figure 6.10). Again, Francesca is caught off guard; just as her perspective becomes more composed and consistent, the view shifts. The use of an ellipsis adds to the measure of dislocation; an elision of Robert's movement from one side of the bridge to the other highlights how his sudden disappearance jars.

The film delicately develops Francesca's 'hide and seek' glances at Robert into a tacit pattern of moves. The call for play comes with the photographer silently taking cover; the game begins with Francesca's response. A touch of apprehension gives way to a quiet smile as she sets off across the bridge once again, to find Robert. Again, the characters stand on different planes, but here the distinction adds to a shared pursuit. Francesca stands above on the bridge pathway, able to spy the stooping photographer gathering flowers below. He positions

Figure 6.10   The Bridges of Madison County (Clint Eastwood, 1995): Camera, no cameraman

himself to be caught in the act. The couple take pleasure and come together in the act of 'catching' each other unawares. True to the principles of hide-and-seek, the act of moving apart prompts not only the pleasure in finding and the relief of being found, but also the thrill of experiencing the outcome of the pursuit together. Here, the point of discovery, of being found, is captured from Francesca's point of view (see Figure 6.11). For the first time, as the camera tilts down to reveal the photographer below, there is the suggestion that Francesca has the advantage. This position is upheld as the game gives way to her teasing suggestion that the flowers are poisonous. Just as quickly, the position of advantage is yielded, giving way to equality. With the release of the bouquet and a peel of laughter, the characters crouch closely together to collect the fallen spray of flowers. In this final moment of release, the couple finds common ground.

The second trip: Holliwell Bridge

Sensitive to the possibilities of variation within repetition, the film handles the second trip, to Holliwell Bridge, to express crucial adjustments in the characters' fledgling relationship. While both the film and characters recognise points of correspondence between the two visits, they are equally alert to senses of development and

Figure 6.11   The Bridges of Madison County (Clint Eastwood, 1995): Robert is caught out

intensification. The second trip affords the couple the opportunity to revisit their shared experience of Roseman Bridge and to move the relationship on, to cover new ground. As the bridges of Madison County become a recurrent meeting place for the couple, they take on particular aspects of familiarity. Like their repeated returns to the Johnson's kitchen, the visits to the bridges become central to the development of the couple's transitory routines. Repetition inspires a reassuring sense of familiarity; in turn, there is an increasing sense of ease. The moves to the bridges also release Francesca from the more established everyday tasks of the family farmhouse. The couple's developing acquaintance, of the setting of the bridge and each other, does not lead to a blasé approach to place and person; rather, it inspires a more intense experience of the linked trips.

The opening shot of Holliwell Bridge encapsulates a fresh sense of readiness and resolve while echoing the first encounter. The bridge is set squarely in the frame amidst high fields (see Figure 6.12). It looks very similar to the bridge of the previous visit. Equally, the framing and distance of the shot recall the opening views of the earlier sequence. Yet there are also crucial distinctions. Unlike the first trip, there is to be no gradual approach. The structure is introduced in

Figure 6.12   The Bridges of Madison County (Clint Eastwood, 1995): Holliwell Bridge

a single static view. Rather than moving nearer to the bridge as the characters do, the film sets Robert's truck in the shot, already stationed by the archway. The immediacy of the view suggests a closer connection between character and setting. This sense is reinforced in a direct cut to Robert in close shot, striding up the bridge's embankment. His position recalls that of the first trip, in his immediate stride down the slope to photograph Roseman Bridge from ground level. Here though, the direction is reversed. Robert moves from the field below towards the bridge mouth, ready to greet and photograph Francesca as she approaches in her truck. While adopting similar positions to the first meeting, camera and character move in.

The second trip's momentum is driven by the direction and directness of the characters' moves towards one another. The drive is emphasised as Francesca's truck rolls promptly through the bridge tunnel. The housewife's tentative steps of the earlier sequence are replaced with a straight passage to Robert. Whereas the characters' earlier alighting from the truck inspired a current of separation, here Francesca steps out of and around the vehicle to shake hands with the waiting photographer. In the meeting on Roseman Bridge, the couple positioned themselves at a remove from each other, to see and be seen with the reassurance of distance. The second trip is marked by a desire for immediate closeness, and for more shared perspectives. An increasing sense of familiarity between the two characters develops alongside their closer relationship with the setting. As they greet, Robert gestures towards the shaded enclave of the bridge, inviting Francesca to 'make [herself] at home'. This neutral space, this place of transition has begun to assume, for these two people, qualities of a familiar shared retreat.

The sense of a closer, more overt connection is promoted in the direction of the camera's attention. At particular points, the film draws together the subject of Robert's lens with that of its own. The sequence begins and ends with repeated close shots of Robert photographing Francesca, positioning her as the true centre of attention, rather than the bridge. The perspective marks a significant change from the first meeting on Roseman Bridge, as previously the film had privileged Francesca's point of view, holding Robert at a distance. The shift in focus conveys Robert's readiness to declare and sustain his interest in Francesca, as well as the housewife's pleasure at being made the subject of his attention.

At other points, the film returns to focus on Francesca's perspective. In turn, and before returning 'home' to the shade of the tunnel, Francesca pauses to watch Robert as he photographs the bridge. Rather than stealing broken glances, she holds her gaze in a sustained gesture of open appreciation. An extensive fluid shot marks the moment, as the camera slowly pans from the housewife, to the man below, and back again. The film commits to the view as Francesca commits to the act of viewing. At the same time, it is important to note that the film does not align the sight with Francesca's optical point of view. Rather, the camera is placed a step away from the character, panning right to note the direction of Francesca's gaze, before following it left to Robert. The decision to refrain from locking together view and eye-line allows the film to convey a gentler act of scrutiny. It notes the moment as one of affectionate interest rather than intrusive surveillance, while retaining the sense of significant connection.

A line of dialogue draws attention to the direction of the characters' perspectives. Nearing the edge of the bridge, Francesca calls for Robert to 'look at that butterfly', floating her hand up towards a point behind the photographer. The words form a request for Robert's attention to meet hers, to share a perspective and point of appreciation. It also expresses a wish to note that her mind is elsewhere, to justify her sustained gaze in the direction of the photographer. She calls for a coupled view, while drawing attention away from her true object of desire.

A moment of open appreciation marks a progression, yet also necessitates retreat. Francesca returns to her more furtive game of hide-and-seek in the body of the bridge. Again the film charts her passage through the tunnel with a series of looks at the photographer below. There is comfort to be found in the clandestine measure and the act of repetition. At the same time, the act of re-*playing* marks a wish to capture again the frisson and thrill of those first stolen views of Robert, on Roseman Bridge.

In the meetings on the bridges, the couple seek to find and complicate senses of familiarity, to draw together and charge their shared time with the stimulation of surprise. This idea reaches its peak in the closing moments of the sequence. Coming to the far edge of the bridge, Francesca leans precariously around the divide to catch a final glimpse of Robert, only to be caught in the act by the photographer, springing from the opposite corner, camera in hand. Again, the characters come together by catching each other unawares. The act of surprising and being surprised engenders a moment of shared delight; the film notes the heightening of the mood in a brisk series of tightly framed portrait shots and a startled Francesca's giddy laughter. Robert's playful approach responds to Francesca's earlier tease of the 'poisonous' bouquet. The joke forms a coda to the two trips, binding the separate meetings together.

The rhyme marks a high point in the couple's relationship. There is the sense that the practical joke, and the trained focus of Robert's camera that serves as a 'punch-line', have been earned, worked for and won in the couple's commitment to spend time together, in their negotiations of the bridges of Madison County. Having composed precise patterns of perspectives, of the characters' viewing and reviewing of the same settings, the film moves the couple into a position of closeness and confidence, in which both figures acknowledge and enjoy the direct attention of the other.

•••

In all of the above instances of position and perspective, grades of spatial proximity are tightly linked with attitudinal characteristics. The particular positions adopted by camera and character express the way they and the film *stand towards* an event. There is a mutuality of consideration between the stance of both, and their points of focus. The organisation of positions and perspectives is of central importance to the ways films convey their viewpoint.

The Age of Innocence orchestrates myriad glimpses and glares. Camera and characters glance at peripheral views and details in larger events. Many such details are positioned spatially on the edge of things; equally, they appear slight in temporal terms, in their transient presence. In other instances, the film intensifies the act of focusing in, of highlighting and scrutinising a detail or happening. At particular points, the film focuses on the direction of the characters' looks. Sometimes the characters directly fix the camera with their gaze. On other occasions, they only appear to do so. Ultimately, aspects of the film's 'focusing in' collect together in a final spell of shots, as Newland concentrates intently on a single shaped memory of Ellen.

The Age of Innocence explores the desire to hold onto particular moments, even as they pass. Conversely, *The Straight Story* handles aspects of focus and viewpoint to express the appreciation of passing details in a wider environment. Glanced details are measured and enjoyed as ephemeral, with the jolt, frisson, or twinge of intensity registered in the moment of discovery passing into a lasting sense of resonance. Both the encounter with the cyclists and the crossing of the Mississippi express Alvin's appreciation of living in the moment. Both are charged with his sense of surprise, pleasure, and perturbation in and of the passing instant. The meaning of a transient event reflects the more momentous implications of Alvin's travels. In both, the film combines optical point-of-view shots matching Alvin's gaze with return shots of his face, and long shots of the setting. In moving between the three viewpoints, the film is able to alter pace and perspective. These alterations grade the transformative aspect of each happening, retaining a sense of intimate association even in the broadest perspectives.

In *The Bridges of Madison County*, camera and character piece together a mosaic of stolen glances and restricted views. As Robert and Francesca seek positions of reassurance, the film explores their shifting perspectives of each other, considering, as they do, where they stand. The film follows the way both *The Straight Story* and *The Age of Innocence* explore their characters' appreciation of place and instant, concentrating on the way they collect glimpses. Yet, whereas the other two films express the joy and pain to be found in considering constantly changing appearances, *The Bridges of Madison County* explores the stimulation possible in repetition. In the lovers' two visits to the bridges, the film details a gradual eroticisation of place, slowly building and burning in a series of looks and touches.

Conclusion

This book has aimed to show that the expansiveness of contemporary Hollywood does not lead, inevitably, to distance and remoteness. Rather, it is a possibility of modern American film to organise its 'big architecture' to render expressions of human closeness. In the four films, expressions of intimacy stem, for example, from sweeping long shots of fields, a mobile phone connection across vast distance, the surging sounds of a song on the radio, the waft of a fan, and an array of exquisite objets d'art. Each film composes a broad canvas of precise patterns, arrangements, and concentrations of detail. The integration and refinement of potentially 'bloated' points of style express the closeness of the characters' relationships. Further, the readings explore how certain expressions of intimacy may be best revealed within an environment of amplitude. For instance, in *The Straight Story*, the connection of Alvin to the land, and the urge and toil of his journey, are encapsulated in a dissolve moving mower across swathes of wheat. In *The Age of Innocence*, the fragile creation of a private, pocketed space is achieved and threatened by its place in the grandiloquent surroundings of a Society dinner. In the expansive worlds of the films, the balance and measure of a scenario conveys the characters' own adjustments, arrangements, and situation. Alert to the pitfalls and possibilities of magnification in the medium of film, the four works conceive sensitive understandings of human affairs.

While being informed by the principles of expressive film criticism, this book redirects a tradition by applying the approach to contemporary Hollywood movies. There appears a resistance in expressive criticism to offer interpretations of modern American film. Correspondingly, there is a belief that contemporary movies resist this kind of treatment. In 1975, V. F. Perkins posited an influential standpoint on modern Hollywood in a round-table discussion for *Movie*. (His comments, then, centre upon an earlier post-studio period than concerns this book; however, they are still pertinent and informative):

> Maybe one could risk a bolder statement by summing up the change in movies since the mid 1960s in terms of the death of *mise en scène*. By that I mean that in my experience of American films of the last five years, the stylistic strategies tend to be either blatantly point-making or to be totally arbitrary choices of what you put where, or what you cross-cut fast or what lens you use. In *Pickup on South Street* (Fuller, 1953) (just because I've seen it recently) there is a rhetoric more or less constantly in play which is nevertheless not a particularly obtrusive rhetoric (one or two points aside). Nowadays I find the strategy of style, the oscillation between point-making and arbitrariness, less and less penetrable compared to the kind of camera placement in *Letter from an Unknown Woman* (Ophuls, 1948) or *On Dangerous Ground* (Ray, 1951).
>
> (1975: 6)

Perkins makes a crucial distinction between the 'rhetoric' of particular films from the classical Hollywood period and that of more recent works. Modern movies are seen to be driven by an 'obtrusive' rhetoric, comprising 'blatantly point-making' or 'arbitrary' choices. In place of earlier achievements in balance and integration comes asserted meaning ('blatantly point-making'). As Perkins states elsewhere, in *Film as Film*, 'Asserted meanings, crude juxtapositions, tend to be both blatant and unclear, like over-amplified noises bellowing from a faulty loudspeaker. When a film's significance is wholly formed at this level it is better described as *imposed* rather than as *contained*' (1972, reprinted 1993: 119). At the same time, other choices in modern movies are seen as 'arbitrary'. Even further divorced from considerations of shape and significance found in *Film as Film*, the organisation of style in the modern film appears randomly devised and arranged. With no correlation of components into significant relationships, the content of the film is rendered crudely.

One can acknowledge that many modern American films display a less than penetrable strategy of style that oscillates between 'point-making and arbitrariness', a strategy beloved of many 'high concept' blockbusters. Equally, however, the interpretations in this book lead to the discernment, in certain Hollywood movies of the 1990s, of significant patterning, intricacies of structure, and qualities of organisation and coherence. Rather than appearing as the equivalents of 'over-amplified noises bellowing from a faulty loudspeaker', grand vistas, imposing landscapes, and elaborate social structures are shaped in precise grades and degrees. Involved tapestries of words, gestures, views, and sounds form delicate patterns.

A close concentration on moments from the four films, across six chapters, enables a breakdown of organisational elements into individual points of style. The act of disassembly reveals the different constituents of the films' architecture. At the same time, the concentration on singular elements shows how different techniques reveal distinct aspects of intimate expression. Moving through the chapters, the book explores some of the most assertive and prominent of the films' visual and aural designs, as well as less demonstrative and more abstract elements. From the majesty of a sweeping vista to the flick of a hand, the elements of style are shaped to convey precise measures and aspects of intimacy.

Chapter 1 addressed the most immediately striking element of a grand-scale film: its arrangement of the landscape, its 'expansive vistas'. Tracts of land and rolling hills carry Alvin to his brother in *The Straight Story*; settings of the Iowan landscape also house the affair between Robert and Francesca in *The Bridges of Madison County*; skyscrapers and grand hotels define the limits of the relationships in *The Insider*; the sumptuous designs of opera houses and ballrooms allow for meetings between lovers in *The Age of Innocence*. The films shape their landscapes to achieve close and complex levels of integration between character and setting. They are alert to the characters' situations in wider environments. At points, the aspect of an expansive space or setting is seen to connect and alter alongside that of the character. The films achieve precise measures of modulation; the landscapes bear and inflect the characters' changing circumstances, and vice versa. The precise intonation of the expressions is distinct across the films. In *The Straight Story*, neither Alvin nor the plight of his personal pilgrimage is 'dwarfed' by the imposing views of the

Iowan countryside. Rather, the film arranges the shifting aspect of the natural landscape to express the moods and meanings of one man's journey. The stretch and undulation of the terrain, while conveying the size of Alvin's task, express the way the character yields and bends to his situation, patiently moving on. The changing light and colour of the landscape, as Alvin waits for the rain to cease, capture a swell of enthusiasm to restart the journey. In contrast, rather than conveying closeness in long shots of its open country spaces, *The Bridges of Madison County* expresses precise grades of enclosure and release in a small number of fixed settings. The porch to the family farmhouse presents Francesca with the openness of the land; at the same time, it draws the family tightly together, away from the inviting prospects of the road. The more impersonal city settings of *The Insider* demand a particular route of the characters' increasingly intimate negotiations. The prescribed associations of grandeur and exclusivity attached to a high-class hotel contain the measures of aloof formality and clandestine disclosure that inform the first meeting of Wigand and Bergman.

Each return to a particular setting – hillside, porch, or hotel – carries the resonance afforded by repetition and variation into an understanding of the characters' relationships. Across the extent of the films, patterns form in cycles: in the motion of wheels and circling shots in *The Straight Story*, marking the rhythm and cohesion of the character's pilgrimage; in each returning view of the spaces of Madison County, expanding and contracting to match the characters' senses of possibility and restriction; to convey Wigand's ongoing and increasing restriction by the surrounding, enclosing structures of his world, as an 'insider'.

The films achieve a balance between the encompassing designs of their landscapes, and the punctuation of the characters' gestures within locales. Without announcing or *pointing at* the significance of individual gestures, the films attend to the impact of a seemingly more diminutive point of style. This consideration formed the focus of Chapter 2. In some instances, the dramatic impetus of a particular scenario is tempered by the austerity of the characters' physical movements. Such is the case in *The Insider*, as the intensity of the men's meetings is contained and measured in their gestures. A sense of containment and control carries in *The Bridges of Madison County*, as Francesca uses the weight and solidity of her surroundings to accommodate little releases of anxiety. The film develops a sense of austerity in Robert's spare gestures. In this instance, the sparseness of gesture creates a sense of strength and gravity. In all cases, the films are alert to the dramatic weight of composure, varying the pitch of a moment in the measure of the characters' moves. At other points, the apparently slight suggestion of a moving hand, head, or body carries the weight of the film. A gesture, when sensitively placed and performed, can encapsulate the mood and meaning of a moment, without appearing mannered or momentous. A tug of Bergman's thumb in *The Insider*, and the tease of a frond of hair in *The Bridges of Madison County* coil and contain a multitude of tensions.

In contrast, the films also conceive declamatory gestures that seek intimacy through varying degrees of affectation. In *The Age of Innocence*, the passing wave of Ellen's fan over throngs of opera-goers forms a personal bewitchment. In the same film, Ellen's audacious move across the room at the Duke of St. Austrey Dinner is publicly demonstrative yet personally weighted, performed to seal her connection with Newland as tightly as a wink of an eye. Across *The Age of Innocence*, public gestures both conceal and allow for a concentration of intimate display. In *The Insider*, Bergman's effusive moves are performed to encourage commitment, to get Wigand to 'open up'. The producer seeks to *sway* the scientist, tempting and taunting in braggadocio moves. Occasionally in the films, the intense assertion of a gesture demands intimacy and risks recoil. In *The Age of Innocence*, as Newland stabs his pen in the air, claiming the afternoon, Ellen shrinks back. In *The Bridges of Madison County*, Robert stands in the rain, wordlessly, hopelessly, declaring his presence to Francesca. In these instances, the films express the possibilities and risks of obtrusive gestures, without appearing overbearing in their own designs.

The films are equally attentive to the rhetoric of the characters' words. The handling of voice and conversation, as addressed in Chapter 3, is indicative of the way bold statements – visual, thematic, and verbal – are refined through arrangements of nuanced expression. Intricate layers of precise articulation shape the dramatic pitch of the films, and carry delicate negotiations between the characters. On the periphery of pronounced public occasions, the lovers in *The Age of Innocence* form private patterns of interrupted conversation. Their relationship achieves a sense of coherence and development through the gradual growth of a chain of words, across disparate spaces and times. In stolen moments, Newland and Ellen compress meaning in brief exchanges, in the precise phrasing of shared words. In contrast, *The Insider* is shown to explore and measure the development of ongoing discussions. Awash with words, the film is sensitive to the length and process of its characters' negotiations. Each exchange is shaped into a crucial stage of passage – from hector to whisper, from joke to caution – forming a verbal equivalent of Alvin's extensive journey in *The Straight Story*. Yet, whereas Alvin is bound by the purpose of his travels but open to the possibilities of the landscape, Wigand and Bergman are tightly restricted in their garrulous meetings. The confidentiality agreement forms an invisible, all-encompassing scaffold to their conversations, at once acting as barrier and support. The two characters find ways to raise issues, on the platform of public concern. Open forms of speculation are addressed in *The Bridges of Madison County*. Like *The Insider*, the film explores the route through ongoing conversations, as expressions move from polite to familiar. The ceremony of polite formality and generality is seen to inspire a quickening of connection between the lovers, as they set off to explore the bridges. In all three films, the wider environment dictates the measure of shared words, and the limitations and possibilities for closeness.

The films take advantage of the resources offered by contemporary technology, without indulging in the easy impact of heightened effects. One crucial example is the use of the range and volume of multi-channel sound in the arrangements of the musical score. Chapter 4 addresses aspects of musical composition in *The Bridges of Madison County* and *The Straight Story*. The former film is shown to shape a single, imposing musical theme in increments and graded variations. Each sounding of the theme marks slight yet crucial shifts in the lovers' relationship. In one particular instance, a moment is transformed by the richness and volume of a song. As Francesca and Robert dance in the kitchen, the film calls upon the scope and scale of its acoustics to fill the screen with the sound of a song. The hypnotic enchantment of the moment is expressed in the low hum of the bass, while stimulation stems from the crispness of the treble. *The Straight Story* broadens the musical range to explore the expanding inferences of multiple themes. In the sounding of 'Rose's Theme', the sight of Rose watching the boy with the ball initially appears peripheral to the greater significances of the film. However, in repetition, the film uses the music of 'Rose's Theme' to bind thematically local moments. As it does so, the momentousness of such a seemingly trivial moment of play emerges. Through the music, in patterns of sound and scenarios, *The Straight Story* creates a gradual deepening of Rose's circumstances. In turn, the significance of these scenarios develops our understanding of Alvin's relationships, from brief encounters with passers-by, to his committed movements to meet with Lyle.

It is a particular achievement of the films that they handle more abstract or non-figurative points of style to express precise measures of human closeness. In Chapter 5, the use of two devices of editing – dissolves and ellipses – is addressed in relation to *The Straight Story* and *The Age of Innocence*. In many narrative films, dissolves and ellipses are employed to 'move the story on', baldly shaving away 'dead' moments of time to sustain the pace and momentum of a plot's designs. The two films considered make use of the devices' capacities of transition and truncation, not only to compress their narratives, but also to measure the bearing and involvement of individual characters in a particular set of circumstances. In *The Straight Story*, through the repeated use of dissolves and ellipses, a prolonged period of travelling is delicately compacted into a much shorter running time. The film is careful to retain a sense of the momentousness of the full journey within the abridged version of events. Each concise moment is created as a scaled-down model of a grander set of circumstances. In this way, the film pockets extensive stretches of time into sequences lasting minutes. Within each sequence (in, for example, Alvin's meeting with Crystal the hitchhiker, and the stopover in the barn), the film uses colour, rhythm, and the recurrence of visual motifs to create a miniature account of a longer period. At the same time, particular condensations carry the full resonance of the character's commitment to a wider set of circumstances. For example, the passage of a dissolve from the mower store to Rose at home expresses a pang of feeling, of Alvin missing his daughter. It strikes a chord, conveying the larger burden of Alvin's prolonged absence from home.

In a corresponding manner, *The Age of Innocence* uses dissolves and ellipses to express the impression that each happening makes on Newland. The film traces across the length and breadth of the world of New York aristocracy, marking time as a series of fashionable and extravagant 'Events'. At the same time, it charts Newland's relationship with Ellen, through the 'Events' and more private rendezvous, and across the years. Through dissolves and ellipses, the film brings both sets of circumstances together. At first, stolen moments of shared time are richly textured, to be savoured as they pass. Ultimately, the expansive world of Society is measured out as a vast, hollow experience for Newland, when he is detached from Ellen. Events and objects shift and slide together as empty tableaux.

A conventional way of expressing the bearing of the world on a film's character is through the use of optical point of view. While being alert to the immediacy afforded by this technique, the films create closer appraisals of intimacy by widening their consideration of perspective. Chapter 6 explored the position and perspective of camera and character in the films' worlds. In a meticulous organisation of viewpoints, the films express the way characters stand towards a particular event. In all of the films considered, optical point of view is used sparingly and at precise points, to convey the immediacy and intensity of a connection. At the same time, the films complicate the conventional associations of point of view shooting to express tensions in the characters' negotiations, of events and each other. In *The Age of Innocence*, POV shots anchor Newland to May, arresting him in her gaze, fixing his wandering eye on his betrothed. At other points, the use of the device expresses a crucial margin of distance, of Ellen to Newland, as she just misses the eye of the camera, and their eye-lines fail to meet. As *The Age of Innocence* channels the viewpoint of the camera to connect character to character, *The Straight Story* uses POV to taper one man's experience of an expansive situation. The pivotal moment of crossing a monumental stretch of water, on reaching the Mississippi, is measured in a series of fragmentary glances from Alvin's perspective. Correspondingly, a charging cascade of cyclists is marked as a pleasurable, personal surprise for Alvin.

The Age of Innocence and *The Straight Story* are equally responsive to the potential significance of the camera's release from optical point of view. In both, a physical broadening of views can retain the signature of a character's personal involvement, while developing the resonance of the moment. In *The Straight Story*, as the camera unlocks from Alvin's perspective to move to a bird's eye view of the cyclists below, it develops (rather than withdraws from) a sense of the character's experience. In *The Age of Innocence*, glances passing between lovers are forever at risk of being intercepted by the flurrying, piercing looks of the collected gentry. In both examples, events 'on the periphery' are surveyed with a sudden intensity of scrutiny. Similarly, Francesca risks being 'discovered' in her stolen glances at Robert. Across the width and breadth of the bridges of Madison County, the characters take pleasure and come together in the act of 'catching' each other, playing an unspoken game of hide-and-seek with their gazes. In the assertive connection of a point-of-view shot to more suggestive glimpses of details at the corners of wider environments, the films' channels of attention convey the characters' shifting commitments.

Focusing each chapter on a particular point of style allows me to channel my attention on particular achievements of the films. At the same time, in revisiting moments through the chapters, the book aims to draw attention to the synthesis of elements within the films. To recall Perkins, 'The specifically filmic qualities derive from the *complex*, not from any one of its components. What distinguishes film from other media, and the fiction movie from other forms, is none of the elements but their combination, interaction, fusion' (1993: 117). In *The Insider*, as Bergman wades into the sea, mobile phone in hand, the resonance of the moment comes from the film's integration of points of style: patterning views of the ocean and hotel, rhyming gestures of the two men as they touch their phones to their ears, pacing the rhythm and trajectory of the characters' words, cutting between shots to suggest Wigand's splintering thoughts and the tempo of Bergman's temper, moving the camera tight to the characters, then at a remove, disconnecting them, leaving Bergman alone in the water's distant shimmer. In the close relationship of points of style, a moment of expansion expresses the precise measures of intimacy achieved, and lost, between the two. In a particularly heightened instance, *The Insider* demonstrates the shared trait of four films' expressive personalities that I have explored in this book: an intricate handling of intimacy on a grand scale.

As well as shaping the complex of their grand designs to convey nuances of the characters' relationships, the films are also alert to tensions and suspensions of meaning. We can recall Klevan's suggestion, as voiced in the Introduction, to be 'responsive to the overlaps, [to] keep in play the balance of meanings' (Gibbs and Pye 2005: 215).

The chapters have explored the balance of association in particular moments of the films. A prominent example is Francesca's trip to Holliwell Bridge, rich in matters of suspension: 'The transient nature of the setting, as an intermediary place between places, matches and promotes the transitory relationship of Robert and Francesca. The conclusion of their time together is undetermined, up in the air.' In *The Age of Innocence*, a meeting of Newland and Ellen occurs under the glare of the gathered crowds and the opera spotlight. As noted, the film's use of narrowed light expresses the intensity of the lovers' feelings for each other. Yet, it can also be viewed as an expression of the intense interest of the surrounding figures. It is a particular achievement of the film to convey both senses at once. In a handling of expansive features, the films create a delicate weighting of suggestion, balancing tensions and complexities of meaning, overlapping concerns.

A concentration on details of the films has allowed for an appreciation of their concentrations *of* details. In each interpretation and discrimination, the book marks an attempt to 'do justice to the visual and aural specifics of a film's expressive personality' (Klevan 2000: 163–4). In doing so, the study brings to light a shared trait of the films' personalities, of their explorations and expressions of 'magnificent intimacy'. These are films of fine-grain control and sensitivity, working in the stylistic amplitude characteristic of contemporary Hollywood. Detailed consideration of this achievement allows for a greater understanding of the designs and possibilities of contemporary cinema. It is hoped that the investigations shared by the reader might develop the critical debates and discriminations surrounding the stylistic relationships of the modern movie.

Notes

Introduction

1. *The Straight Story*, production by Walt Disney Pictures, distribution by Buena Vista Productions; *The Bridges of Madison County*, production by Amblin/Malpaso, distribution by Warner Bros; *The Age of Innocence*, production and distribution by Columbia Pictures; *The Insider*, production by Touchstone Pictures, distribution by Buena Vista.

2. Online and newspaper film reviews often provide such assertions about modern works. On *The Last King of Scotland*'s (Kevin Macdonald, 2006) depiction of Idi Amin, Chad Webb (2008) claims that 'Despite its uncanny brutality, *The Last King of Scotland* is a severely intimate picture. Director Kevin Macdonald devises this tale in a way that impeccably displays the dictator's development from enchanting to malicious'. Film critic of *The Evening Standard* Derek Malcolm (2008) praises *Atonement* (Joe Wright, 2007) from a similar perspective, declaring that '[A]n intimate portrait of three intertwining lives is its ultimate triumph'. For a persuasive study of the viewer's close relationships with people in film, see Murray Smith (1995) and Jens Eder (2006).

3. The source for *The Insider* is Marie Brenner (1996). One report on the factual origins of *The Straight Story* is provided by Martha P. Nochimson (2000). The source novels for the other two films are by Robert James Waller (1992) and Edith Wharton (1948). For a comparative account of book and film versions of *The Bridges of Madison County* see Richard Alleva (1995) and Walter Metz (1997). For corresponding articles on *The Age of Innocence* see Philip Horne (1998) and Karli Lukas (2003).

4. See, for example, V. F. Perkins's work on this film across different publications (1982; 2000a; 2000b) and Robin Wood's various contributions (1991; 2003). Also notable are George M. Wilson (1986), Alexander Dhoest (2003), and Steve Neale (2005).

5. Martin places three of the four directors into his groupings. Clint Eastwood is seen as a classical director, Michael Mann as expressionist, while Martin Scorsese works with a film style that 'virtually functions on all three tiers simultaneously' (1990: 4). Elsewhere, Martin describes Eastwood as 'a sublimely classical director', and notes, on Scorsese, he is 'right at the trembling edge of the classical style: there is just enough of a shred of continuity left before the scene splinters into modernist chaos' (2004: 10).

6. See, for example: Leslie Stern (1995) on *The Age of Innocence*; John Gibbs (2001; 2006) on *Lone Star*, *Unforgiven*, and *Candyman*; Deborah Thomas (2001) on *Schindler's List*; Ed Gallafent (1994) on *Unforgiven*; and Andrew Klevan (1998) on *Titanic*.

7. See, for example, Murray Smith, 'Theses on the Philosophy of Hollywood History', in Steve Neale and Murray Smith (eds) (2000: 3–20), and Richard Maltby, '"Nobody Knows Everything": Post-Classical Historiographies and Consolidated Entertainment' (ibid.: 21–44). Elsewhere, indicative writings include Myros Konstankarakos (2002), and Barry Salt (1992).

8. See Douglas Gomery, 'Hollywood Corporate Business Practice and Periodizing Contemporary Film History', in Neale and Smith (eds) (2000: 47–57), and Tino Balio, '"A Major Presence in All the World's Important Markets": The Globalisation of Hollywood in the 1990s' (ibid.: 58–73). See also Justin Wyatt (1994).

9. Many scholars are involved in explorations of the effect and affect of a 'technology of effects' on forms of narrative. See, for example, Geoff King (2000). Others negotiate aspects of 'specularity' engendered by current forms of technology on and in film: see Warren Buckland, 'Realism in the Photographic and Digital Image (*Jurassic Park* and *The Lost World*)', in Warren Buckland and Thomas Elsaesser (2002: 195–219).

10. This grouping accommodates Reception Studies, as well as cognitive and epistemological approaches to contemporary Hollywood film. See Janet Staiger (2000); Ed S. Tan (1996); and Warren Buckland and Thomas Elsaesser, 'Cognitive Theories of Narration', in Warren Buckland and Thomas Elsaesser (2002: 168–194).

11. Indicative in this respect is the predominant slant of popular British film journal *Sight and Sound* (London, BFI). See, for example, Amy Taubin's 1999 piece in *Sight and Sound* on a film that has since become, for many, the case-study contemporary Hollywood film *sine qua non* for socio-cultural readings: *Fight Club* (David Fincher, 1999). Taubin remarks how 'What's exciting about *Fight Club* is that it "screws around with your bio-rhythms" – to borrow a phrase from the Chuck Palahniuk novel of the same name which has been adapted with considerable fidelity by Fincher and screenwriter Jim Uhls. Like the novel, the film disrupts narrative sequencing and expresses some pretty subversive, right-on-the-zeitgeist ideas about masculinity and our name-brand, bottom-line society – ideas you're unlikely to find so openly broadcast in any other Hollywood movie. "Self-improvement is masturbation. Self-destruction might be the answer" is the slogan of Tyler Durden, who is not *Fight Club*'s protagonist but rather the protagonist's significant other, *doppelgänger*, alter-ego – all that and more. Tyler is the embodiment of pure id with just enough Nietzsche thrown in to make him articulate. (In the film Tyler's voice trails off after the word 'destruction', which he delivers with a pregnant, upward inflection and Cheshire-cat grin. The alteration to the line is, I suspect, a concession to the MPAA ratings board, which probably gave *Fight Club* an 'R' because its members didn't understand its 'unamerican' social critique)' (1999 online article http://www.bfi.org.uk/sightandsound/feature/193).

1   Place and Patterning

1. The effect is repeated elsewhere in the film. As Alvin sets up camp in the Riordans' backyard, the friendly couple brighten up his shelter with colourful wooden decorations. With the camera positioned close to the shelter's canopy, a long shot lays one of the delicate adornments over an image of the family home, looming black in the distance. As with the mower-wheel, Alvin's presence shapes the views of a familiar setting. As he remarks to Danny Riordan (James Cada), 'you'll be a stranger in your own backyard'.

2. The moment takes its place in a wider pattern: in moments of uncertainty, Francesca presses herself tight to the rigid markers of her surroundings, on the struts of the porch, under the arch of the bridges, in the farmhouse. Later in the film, returning to the house with her husband after a final, silent farewell to Robert, Francesca tucks herself into the nook of the kitchen pantry, hiding as if seeking to meld with the fixings of the house, finally giving herself over to her life's inflexible structures.

3. As the affair grows to a close, the couple choose to change routine and setting, to eat their last meal together in the dining room. Scarcely seen or used, the space is laden with the rituals and ceremony of more reserved gatherings, of lighting candles and setting places. The formality of the setting chimes with the stiffness of the last meeting; there is no *give* in this room.

2   Gesture

1. Richard Alleva represents this camp most succinctly when he writes, in *Commonweal*, 'the dialogue is ludicrous, the rummaging in trunks and chit-chat with the lawyers tedious, and the acting of Victor Slezak as Francesca's son risible' (1995: 17).

2. In suggesting the elusive aspects of a lone drifter, Eastwood as director addresses the screen persona of Eastwood as star and 'Stranger'. Richard Combs sees *The Bridges of Madison County* as a 'fascinating experiment', in its handling of the established persona: 'It's the glamorous photographer, of course, who comes from nowhere, preceded by all the men with no name, high plains drifters, and pale riders. Eastwood has consistently treated these figures as spectres appearing to answer to need, then disappearing because nothing real could hold them. Their ghostliness testifies to the sense of the absurd that a reasonable, realistic man has about his glamorous profession. But *Bridges* is a fascinating experiment in taking this will o' the wisp out of genre mythology and putting him in a psychologically realistic scenario, where the supernatural agent, the spiritual liberator, also looks like a spiritual raider … Francesca at one point mocks him as that, when she speculates how he is free to move on to his next four-day liaison: 'the world citizen … who experiences everything and nothing at the same time … someone who doesn't need meaning, he just goes with the mystery' (1996: 30). For further

inquiry into the ethereal qualities of Eastwood as 'Stranger', see Edward Gallafent (1994: 7–11, 112–19, 130–7). Alert to the glamour and mythology surrounding the persona, *The Bridges of Madison County* tempers these qualities into wisps of rarity and curiosity.

3. 'The Shaughraun': an operatic play by Dion Boucicault (1874).
4. An earlier version of this passage of writing, on Olenska's gestures at the Opera and Ball, appears in the article 'Holding onto Moments in *The Age of Innocence*' (Peacock 2006).
5. Accordingly, Damon Wise asks 'Can Hollywood's big acting get any bigger?' wryly citing Day Lewis's performance in *There Will Be Blood* (Paul Thomas Anderson, 2008) as the apogee of such 'big acting': 'His performance – or rather behaviour – in *There Will Be Blood* puts the tin hat on everything. It doesn't just dominate the film, it IS the film, and while watching him deliver the near three-hour film's climactic monologue it's possible to speculate whether any other acting was done elsewhere in the world that day, because Dan looks like he's doing it ALL' (2008: 8).

3 Voice and Conversation

1. The intricacies and achievements of the use of the narrator's voice in *The Age of Innocence* have been considered elsewhere, in detail, by Deborah Thomas. In her article 'The Age of Innocence', Thomas explores the way the narrator's voice enhances the film's expressions of closeness and distance. Thomas details the precise arrangements of the voice, in terms of its appearance and absence at particular points and in relation to particular characters, its complications of irony and compassion, and notions of the narrator's 'reliability' (2001: 22–33).

4 Music

1. The theme is listed as 'Doe Eyes' on the CD soundtrack of the film, and is composed by Clint Eastwood, 'Music from the Motion Picture *The Bridges of Madison County*', Warner Music, 1995.
2. Dinah Washington, 'Blue Gardenia' (written by Bob Russell and Lester Lee), as listed on the CD soundtrack of the film (ibid.).
3. Johnny Hartman, 'I See Your Face Before Me', written by Howard Dietz and Arthur Schwartz (ibid.).
4. As listed on the CD soundtrack of *The Straight Story* (1999, produced by David Lynch and Angelo Badalamenti, released by Windham Hill).

5 Dissolve and Ellipsis

1. After a number of 'incidental' tête-à-têtes (at Mrs Mingott's house, at dinner), the seemingly ingenuous May dispatches a letter to Ellen, announcing her hastened wedding date. The announcement appears to come

before Newland is himself informed. (Wryly, Newland discovers the news during one of his own private meetings with Ellen.) Later, May hints at the most influential of her 'wonderful talks' with Ellen in a couple of passing asides to her husband. Unbeknownst to Newland, May has revealed her certainty that she is pregnant, to Ellen. *How* she chooses to declare this excoriating confidence to Ellen remains occluded. The announcement leads to the removal of the Countess from New York Society, away from Newland.

2. In 'Time's Covetousness', Leslie Stern describes another scene in the film thus, as Newland delicately removes Ellen's glove in a stolen moment 'in carriage': 'Through a series of dissolves he takes one of his gloves off and touches a pearl button on her wrist. The buttons are undone. Prising apart the glove's opening he sinks his face into the inside of her wrist. A momentary ceremonial' (1995: 225).

3. In the same vein, Mrs Mingott presses upon May the necessity of having her hands sculpted by 'the great Rochet'. This May dutifully performs, as one essential stop on the honeymoon trip.

4. Martin Scorsese provides an insightful passage of commentary to further this notion: 'Later on I figured out that as she gets up from the chair we should do it in three cuts, three separate close-ups because I think he'll never forget that moment for the rest of his life. I think he'll play it back many times. When she gets up I thought we should play it back like a memory. It's a medium shot, then a shot of her coming into the frame, and then a third one – she almost grows in stature. It's just his perception, his memory of what it's going to be like.' Taken from 'Street Smart: an Interview with Martin Scorsese', Gavin Smith (1998: 72).

6 Position and Perspective

1. This description of Lefferts comes from the narrator's collection of passing asides during the Beaufort Ball.

2. At the end of Act 1, the sister of an Irish wanderer (the Shaughraun) discovers the man she loves is an English officer sent to kill her brother.

Filmography

The following abbreviations have been used:

d	director	*ed*	editor
m	music	*n*	novel
p	producer	*pd*	production design
ph	cinematographer	*s*	story
sc	scriptwriter		

The Age of Innocence

1993 United States colour 139 minutes
p Barbara De Fina *d* Martin Scorsese *sc* Jay Cocks, Martin Scorsese *n* Edith Wharton *ph* Michael Ballhaus *ed* Thelma Schoonmaker *pd* Dante Ferretti *m* Elmer Bernstein *cast* Daniel Day-Lewis (*Newland Archer*), Michelle Pfeiffer (*Ellen Olenska*), Winona Ryder (*May Welland*), Alexis Smith (*Louise van der Luyden*), Geraldine Chaplin (*Mrs Welland*), Mary Beth Hurt (*Regina Beaufort*), Alec McCowen (*Sillerton Jackson*), Richard E. Grant (*Larry Lefferts*), Miriam Margolyes (*Mrs Mingott*), Robert Sean Leonard (*Ted Archer*), Sian Phillips (*Mrs Archer*), Jonathan Pryce (*Monsieur Rivière*), Michael Gough (*Henry van der Luyden*), Joanne Woodward (*Narrator*).

The Bridges of Madison County

1995 United States colour 135 minutes
p, d, m Clint Eastwood *sc* Richard LaGravenese *n* Robert James Waller *ph* Jack N. Green *ed* Joel Cox *pd* Jeannine Claudia Oppenwall *cast* Clint Eastwood (*Robert Kincaid*), Meryl Streep (*Francesca Johnson*), Annie Corley (*Carolyn Johnson*), Victor Slezak (*Michael Johnson*), Jim Haynie (*Richard Johnson*), Sarah Kathyrn Schmitt (*Young Carolyn*), Christopher Kroon (*Young Michael*), Phyllis Lyons (*Betty*), Debra Monk (*Madge*), Richard Lage (*Lawyer*), Michelle Benes (*Lucy Redfield*).

The Insider

1999 United States colour 157 minutes
p Pieter Jan Brugge *d* Michael Mann *sc* Eli Roth, Michael Mann *ph* Dante Spinotti *ed* William Goldenberg *pd* Brian Morris *m* Pieter Bourke *cast* Al Pacino (*Lowell Bergman*), Russell Crowe (*Jeffrey Wigand*), Christopher

Plummer (*Mike Wallace*), Diana Venora (*Liane Wigand*), Philip Baker Hall (*Don Hewitt*), Hallie Kate Eisenberg (*Barbara Wigand*).

The Straight Story

1999 United States colour 112 minutes
p Pierre Edelman *d* David Lynch *sc* John Roach, Mary Sweeney *ph* Freddie Francis *ed* Mary Sweeney *pd* Jack Fisk *m* Angelo Badalamenti *cast* Richard Farnsworth (*Alvin Straight*), Sissy Spacek (*Rose Straight*), Jane Galloway Heitz (*Dorothy*), Joseph A. Carpenter (*Bud*), Dan Flannery (*Doctor Gibbons*), Everett McGill (*Tom*), Anastasia Webb (*Crystal*), James Cada (*Danny Riordan*), Sally Wingert (*Darla Riordan*), Wiley Harker (*Verlyn Heller*), Kevin P. Farley (*Harold Olsen*), John Farley (*Thorvald Olsen*), Harry Dean Stanton (*Lyle Straight*).

Extended filmography

Amistad (Steven Spielberg, 1997)
Apollo 13 (Ron Howard, 1995)
Armageddon (Michael Bay, 1998)
Atonement (Joe Wright, 2007)
Candyman (Bernard Rose, 1992)
Crow, The (Alex Proyas, 1994)
Easy Rider (Dennis Hopper, 1961)
Every Which Way But Loose (James Fargo, 1978)
Fight Club (David Fincher, 1999)
Heat (Michael Mann, 1995)
It's a Wonderful Life (Frank Capra, 1946)
Jerry Maguire (Cameron Crowe, 1996)
Jungle Fever (Spike Lee, 1991)
Jurassic Park (Steven Spielberg, 1993)
Last King of Scotland, The (Kevin Macdonald, 2006)
Letter from an Unknown Woman (Max Ophuls, 1948)
Lone Star (John Sayles, 1996)
Lost Highway (David Lynch, 1997)
Lost World, The: Jurassic Park (Steven Spielberg, 1997)
Love Me Tender (Robert D. Webb, 1956)
Magnificent Ambersons, The (Orson Welles, 1942)
Magnolia (Paul Thomas Anderson, 1999)
Mariachi, El (Robert Rodriguez, 1992)
On Dangerous Ground (Nicholas Ray, 1951)
Philadelphia Story, The (George Kukor, 1940)
Pick-up on South Street (Samuel Fuller, 1953)
Psycho (Alfred Hitchcock, 1960)
Rain Man (Barry Levinson, 1988)
Scarlet Empress, The (Josef von Sternberg, 1934)

Schindler's List (Steven Spielberg, 1993)
Searchers, The (John Ford, 1956)
Sleepy Hollow (Tim Burton, 1999)
South Park: Bigger, Longer & Uncut (Trey Parker, 1999)
There Will Be Blood (Paul Thomas Anderson, 2008)
Titanic (James Cameron, 1997)
Touch of Evil (Orson Welles, 1958)
Two-Lane Blacktop (Monte Hellman, 1971)
Unforgiven (Clint Eastwood, 1992)
U-Turn (Oliver Stone, 1997)
Wall Street (Oliver Stone, 1987)
Wild at Heart (David Lynch, 1990)

Bibliography

Alleva, R. (1995) 'The Bridges of Madison County', Commonweal, 122, 13–17.

Arroyo, J. (2000) Action/Spectacle Cinema: A Sight and Sound Reader. London: BFI.

Bingham, D. (1994) Acting Male: Masculinity in the Films of James Stewart, John Wayne and Clint Eastwood. New Jersey: Rutgers University Press.

Bordwell, D. (2006) The Way Hollywood Tells It: Story and Style in Modern Movies. London, Berkeley and California: University of California Press.

Buckland, W. and T. Elsaesser (2002) Studying Contemporary American Film: A Guide to Movie Analysis. London: Hodder Arnold.

Buscombe, E. (2000) The Searchers. London: BFI.

Cardullo, B. (2004) In Search of Cinema: Writings on International Film Art. London: McGill-Queen's University Press.

Combs, R. (1996) 'Old Ghosts: The Bridges of Madison County', Film Comment, 32, 3, 25–32.

Davies, J. and C. R. Smith (1997) Gender, Ethnicity and Sexuality in Contemporary American Film. Keele: BAAS Publications.

Davis. J. L. (1993) 'The Rituals of Dining in Edith Wharton's The Age of Innocence', Midwest Quarterly, 34, 4, 471–2.

Davison, A and E. Sheen (2004) The Cinema of David Lynch: American Dreams, Nightmare Visions. London and New York: Wallflower Press.

De Botton, A. (2003) The Art of Travel. London: Penguin.

Durgnat, R. (2002) A Long Hard Look at Psycho. London: BFI.

Eder, J. (2006) 'Ways of being close to characters', Film Studies, 8, 68–80.

Farber, M. (1971) Negative Space: Manny Farber on the Movies. London: Studio Vista.

Gallafent, E. (1994) Clint Eastwood: Actor and Director. London: Studio Vista.

Gibbs, J. (2001) Mise-en-scène: Film Style and Interpretation. London: Wallflower Press.

—— (2006) 'Filmmakers' Choices', Close-Up 01. London: Wallflower Press, 1–88.

—— and D. Pye (2005) Style and Meaning: Studies in the Detailed Analysis of Film. Manchester: Manchester University Press.

Gomery, D. (2000) 'Hollywood Corporate Business Practice and Periodizing Contemporary Film History', in S. Neale and M. Smith (eds), Contemporary Hollywood Cinema. London and New York: Routledge, 52–7.

Hall, S. (2002) 'Tall Revenue Features: The Genealogy of the Modern Blockbuster', in S. Neale (ed.), Genre and Contemporary Hollywood. London: BFI, 23–9.

Horne, P. (1998) 'The James Gang', Sight and Sound, 8, 1, 19–21.

James, N. (2002) Heat. London: BFI.

Jones, K. (2000) 'White Noise', Film Comment, 35, 7, 33.

Kauffmann, S. (1999) '*The Straight Story*', *The New Republic*, 4426, 28.

King, G. (2000) *Spectacular Narratives: Hollywood in the Age of the Blockbuster*. London: I. B. Tauris.

Klevan, A. (1998) '*Titanic*: James Cameron, 1997', *Mortality*, 3, 3, 307–8.

—— (2000) 'The mysterious disappearance of style: Some critical notes about the writing on *Dead Ringers*', in M. Grant (ed.), *The Modern Fantastic: The Films of David Cronenberg*. Trowbridge: Flicks Books.

—— (2005) *Film Performance: From Achievement to Appreciation*. London: Wallflower Press.

Kostankarakos, M. (2002) *New Cinemas: A Journal of Contemporary Film*. Bristol: Intellect Books.

Lee, A. R. (2000) 'Watching Manners: Martin Scorsese's *The Age of Innocence*, Edith Wharton's *The Age of Innocence*', in R. Gidding and E. Sheen (eds), *The Classic Novel: From Page to Screen*. Manchester: Manchester University Press, 171–81.

Lewis, J. (2001) *The End of Cinema As We Know It: American Film in the Nineties*. New York: New York University Press.

Martin, A. (1990) '*Mise-en-scène* is dead, or The Expressive, The Excessive, The Technical and The Stylish', *Continuum*, 5, 2, 87–140.

—— (2004) 'Placing *Mise en Scène*: An Argument with John Gibbs', *Mise-en-Scène, Film Philosophy*, 8, 20, 10–21.

Metz, W. (1997) '"Another being we have created called 'us'": Point of View, Melancholia, and the Joking Unconscious in The Bridges of Madison County', *The Velvet Light Trap*, 39, 66–83.

Miller, T. (2001) *Global Hollywood*. London: BFI.

Neale, S. and M. Smith (2000) *Contemporary Hollywood Cinema*. London and New York: Routledge.

—— (2005) 'Narration, point of view and patterns in the soundtrack of *Letter from an Unknown Woman* (Max Ophuls, 1948)', in J. Gibbs and D. Pye (eds), *Style and Meaning: Studies in the Detailed Analysis of Film*. Manchester: Manchester University Press, 98–107.

Orr, J. (1998) *Contemporary Cinema*. Edinburgh: Edinburgh University Press.

Peacock, S. (2006) 'Holding onto Moments in *The Age of Innocence*', *Film Studies: an International Review*. Manchester: Manchester University Press, 40–50.

—— (2010) *Colour*. Manchester: Manchester University Press.

Perez, G. (1998) *The Material Ghost: Films and their Medium*. Baltimore and London: The Johns Hopkins University Press.

Perkins, V. F., Ian Cameron, Michael Walker, Jim Hillier, and Robin Wood (1975) 'The Return of *Movie*', *Movie*, 20, 1–6.

—— (1982) '*Letter from an Unknown Woman*', *Movie*, 29/30, 61–72.

—— (1990) *The Magnificent Ambersons*. London: BFI.

—— (1993) *Film as Film: Understanding and Judging Movies*. London and New York: Da Capo Press [first published in 1972].

—— (2000a) 'Ophuls contra Wagner and Others', *Movie*, 36, 57–64.

—— (2000b) '"Same Tune Again!" – Repetition and Framing in *Letter from an Unknown Woman*', *CineAction*, 52.

Phillips, A. (2000) *On Flirtation*. London: Faber and Faber.

Romao, T. (1999) 'The International Cinema of Poetry', *Film-Philosophy*, 3, 49, 1–5.

Rothman, W. (1998) *The 'I' of the Camera: Essays in Film Criticism, History and Aesthetics*. Cambridge: Cambridge University Press.

Salt, B. (1992) *Film Style and Technology: History and Analysis*. London: Starwood.

Smith, G. (1998) 'Street Smart: An Interview with Martin Scorsese', *Film Comment*, 34, 3, 69–74.

—— (1999) 'Inside Out', *Film Comment*, 35, 5, 58.

Smith, M. (1995) *Engaging Characters: Fiction, Emotion and the Cinema*. London: Clarendon Press.

Staiger, J. (2000) *Perverse Spectators: The Practice of Film Reception*. New York: New York University Press.

Sterne, L. (1995) *The Scorsese Connection*. Bloomington and Indianapolis: Indiana University Press.

Tan, E. S. (1996) *Emotion and the Structure of Narrative Film: Film as an Emotion Machine*. London: Routledge.

Taubin, A. (1999) 'Dread and Desire', *Sight and Sound*, 3, 12, 9.

Thomas, D. (2001) *Reading Hollywood: Spaces and Meanings in American Film*. London: Wallflower Press.

Thomson, D. (1994) *The New Biographical Dictionary of Film*, Revised and enlarged edition. London: André Deutsch.

Tobler, J. (2001) *Art USA*. London: Phaidon Press.

Waller, R. J. (1992) *The Bridges of Madison County*. New York: Warner Books.

Wharton, E. (1948) *The Age of Innocence*. New York: Appleton Century.

Willis, S. (1997) *High Contrast: Race and Gender in Contemporary Hollywood Film*. Durham and London: Duke University Press.

Wilson, G. M. (1986) 'Max Ophuls' *Letter from an Unknown Woman*', *Narration in Light: Studies in Cinematic Point of View*. Baltimore and London: The John Hopkins University Press, 103–25.

Wise, D. (2008) 'More is more', *The Guardian Weekend Edition: Review*, 7–8.

Wood, R. (1976) *Personal Views: Explorations in Film*. London: Gordon Fraser.

—— (1991) 'Ewig hin der Liebe Glück', in V. W. Wexman and K. Holling (eds), *Letter from an Unknown Woman*. New Jersey: Rutgers University Press, 220–36.

—— (2003) '*Letter from an Unknown Woman*: The Double Narrative', *CineAction*, 31, 4–17.

Wyatt, J. (1994) *High Concept: Movies and Marketing in Hollywood*. Austin: University of Texas Press.

Online sources

Brenner, M. (1996) 'The Man Who Knew Too Much', *Vanity Fair*, www.mariebrenner.com. Accessed on 4 July, 2002. http://www.mariebrenner.com/content/other_writing.asp#themanwhoknewtoomuch.

Dhoest, A. (2003) 'Ophuls Conducting: Music and Musicality in *Letter from an Unknown Woman*', *Senses of Cinema*, 28, www.sensesofcinema.com. Accessed on 25 July, 2008. http://www.sensesofcinema.com/2003/28/music_letter_from_unknown_woman/.

Honeycutt, K. (2005) '*XXX: State of the Union*', *Hollywood Reporter*, www.hollywoodreporter.com. Accessed on 25 July, 2008. http://www.fandango.com/xxx:stateoftheunion_85883/criticreviews.

Howe, D. (1993) '*The Age of Innocence*', *The Washington Post*, www.washingtonpost.com. Accessed on 23 July, 2008. http://www.washingtonpost.com/wp-srv/style/longterm/movies/videos/theageofinnocencepghowe_a0aff3.htm.

Kay, B. (2006) '*Troy*', www.flixnjoystix.com. Accessed on 18 May, 2007. Site now expired.

Lukas, K. (2003) 'Creative Visions: (De)Constructing "The Beautiful" in Scorsese's *The Age of Innocence*', *Senses of Cinema*, www.sensesofcinema.com, 25. Accessed on 14 July, 2008. http://www.sensesofcinema.com/2003/cteq/age_of_innocence/.

Malcolm, D. (2008) '*Atonement*', *The Evening Standard*, www.thisislondon.co.uk. Accessed on 29 August, 2008. http://www.thisislondon.co.uk/film/Derek%20Malcolm-critic-4-archive.do.

Martin, A. (2000) 'Delirious Enchantment', *Senses of Cinema*, www.sensesofcinema.com, 1, 5. Accessed on 20 June, 2004. http://archive.sensesofcinema.com/contents/00/5/index.html.

Morris, W. (1999) 'Lynch goes magically, touchingly, "straight"', *The San Francisco Chronicle*, www.sfgate.com. Accessed on 20 October, 2000. http://www.sfgate.com/cgi-bin/article.cgi?f=/e/a/1999/10/22/WEEKEND893.dtl.

Nochimson, M. (2000) '*The Straight Story*: Sunlight Will Out of Darkness Come', *Senses of Cinema*, www.sensesofcinema.com, 7. Accessed on 29 August, 2008. http://archive.sensesofcinema.com/contents/00/7/straight.html.

Taubin, A. (1999) 'So Good it Hurts: *Fight Club*', *Sight and Sound*, www.bfi.org.uk/sightandsound, November 1999 issue. Accessed on 20 July, 2010. http://www.bfi.org.uk/sightandsound/feature/193.

Thoret, J. (2002) 'The Aquarium Syndrome: On the Films of Michael Mann', *Senses of Cinema*, www.sensesofcinema.com, 19. Accessed on 20 May, 2007. http://www.sensesofcinema.com/contents/01/19/mann/html.

Webb, C. (2008) '*The Last King of Scotland*', www.411mania.com. Accessed on 29 August, 2008. http://www.411mania.com/movies/film_reviews/46013/The-Last-King-of-Scotland-Review.html.

Index